CHESSINGTO[

GW00646806

REMEMBERED

*F*OR *many people, Chessington is synonymous with the zoo. But there is far more to the district than the World of Adventures. Take a trip down memory lane and peep beyond the concrete and mortar of the pre- and post-war estates. You will discover another world of adventures in a delightful rural setting. Here, in these pages, re-live a life in a little community set among dairy farms, hay fields and meadows. Discover what it was like to be in a tiny village called Chessington before the developers moved in. In this other world, milk was brought to your doorstep and ladled into jugs; the post office was in someone's front room and the bus to school was a farm cart pulled by a horse. Today, pockets of rural Chessington still survive and are a pleasant reminder of a past age. Now take a roller coaster ride through the decades to see for yourself the Chessington of old ...*

Old Forge tea rooms owner Mrs W Mackay was left for dead when a well-spoken robber hit her over the head with a life preservative and stole £3 10s from her purse in October 1934. In the 1990s, the former cafe sold double glazing.

Reginald Goddard, who founded Chessington Zoo in 1931 after realising that pets drew large crowds. In just a few weeks he had the zoo up and running and thousands of people were soon passing through the turnstiles.

1

Chessington PO

THE first post office in Chessington appears to have been in Leatherhead Road, next to the village's first school. This was next to Court Cottages, 100 yards from today's Mansfield Road. The building has gone but the cottages are still standing. In 1851, the postmaster was James Cooper. By 1855, however, the post office is not listed in the record books but is shown on an 1866 map as being next to the old school.

In 1890, George Taylor is listed as the postmaster and he traded, it is thought, at Post Office Row, Leatherhead Road, opposite the Garrison Lane junction. The cottage housing the PO is now Barwell Cafe. The rest of Post Office Row has long since disappeared. In 1902, the post was collected at 9.30am, 3.20pm and 6.30pm. On Sundays, the mail was picked up at 9.15am.

Mr Taylor, also a greengrocer, continued in this role until 1914, when trading transferred to a detached cottage in Leatherhead Road next to Chessington Garage, just south of the Oxshott side of the Fairoak Lane crossroads. It is pictured, left, and was demolished in the early 1960s. In the 1990s, the Mole Valley Motors' TVR garage traded where the cottage once stood. Mrs Mary Cole was the sub-postmistress assisted by her husband, George James William Cole.

From 1926 to 1930, Mrs Elizabeth Sayers, a short, rosy-cheeked woman, ran the post office from the front room of her family home at Almond Tree Cottages, (now No. 378 Leatherhead Road and the home for many years of Thelma and Jess James). It was next to the Fair Oak Brickyard and Potteries.

By 1931, Fair Oaks, a house on the other side of the road, at the crossroads, became the PO stores and cafe. By 1934, Gilders Road post office had opened. Fairoak Lane PO closed in 1989 and its shop soon after.

Mary Cole's Chessington post office, Leatherhead Road, c1914.

Acknowledgements

Dennis Stickley, Paul Adams, St Mary's Church PCC, Rev and Mrs Flynn; Ted Moore, Reg Driver, Mark Barker, Jim Watling, Ann Foy, Evelyn Rapley, Marjorie Martin, Marion Bone, Ros Fryer, Surrey History Centre, Tim Everson and Jill Lamb at Kingston Museum and Heritage Centre, Norman, Muriel and Nigel Davison, Joan Clark, Vera Quigley, the Foster family; Betty Rhodes, Betty Odell, Doris Westwood, Ann Sayers, Margaret Hobbs, Raymond Kelsey, Carol Hill, Jeremy Hart and Bourne Hall Museum; Mr Tims of Fetcham, staff at all the Chessington schools, Mr and Mrs B Woodall, Bert Broom, St Catherine's Church, Tony Sherwin, Barbara Childs, Kingston Museum Wheatfield Way staff; the late Margaret Bellars; Les Stitson and the London Omnibus Traction Society. Arthur Moyle, Roger Vaughan, Petula Clark, Dave Swan, Tomas Holy.

Photograph credits

Kingston Museum and Heritage Centre, British Museum, David Tippett-Wilson archives, John Tims collection, Surrey Comet, D Stickley collection, Mark Davison collection, Kingston Borough News archives, St Mary's Church and PCC, Hilda Pratt, Ann Sayers, Margaret Hobbs, Tony Sherwin, Surrey History Centre, the late Betty Smith of Hook, Betty Odell, Paul Adams archives, Joan Clark, Daily Sketch, Mary Foster collection, Ellingham, Moor Lane and Lovelace schools, Surrey Postal History Society.

Bibliography

Notes on the History of Chessington by D J Field; Bryan Randell's unpublished Chessington research; The Chessington Story by C H Keeling, Kingston Then and Now by Margaret Bellars, Hook Remembered by Mark Davison, The Story of Hook In Kingston, by Marion Bone, Surrey Comet, Kingston Borough News, London Suburban Railways: Wimbledon to Epsom, by Vic Mitchell and Keith Smith.

© Copyright October 1999

Published by Mark Davison, North Bank, Smoke Lane, Reigate, Surrey, RH2 7HJ

Printed by Litho Techniques (Kenley), Godstone Road, Whyteleafe, Surrey CR3 OEA

ISBN 0 - 9534240-1-4

A special thanks to:

Rev Peter Flynn

Mary Foster

D. Tippett-Wilson

Hilda Pratt

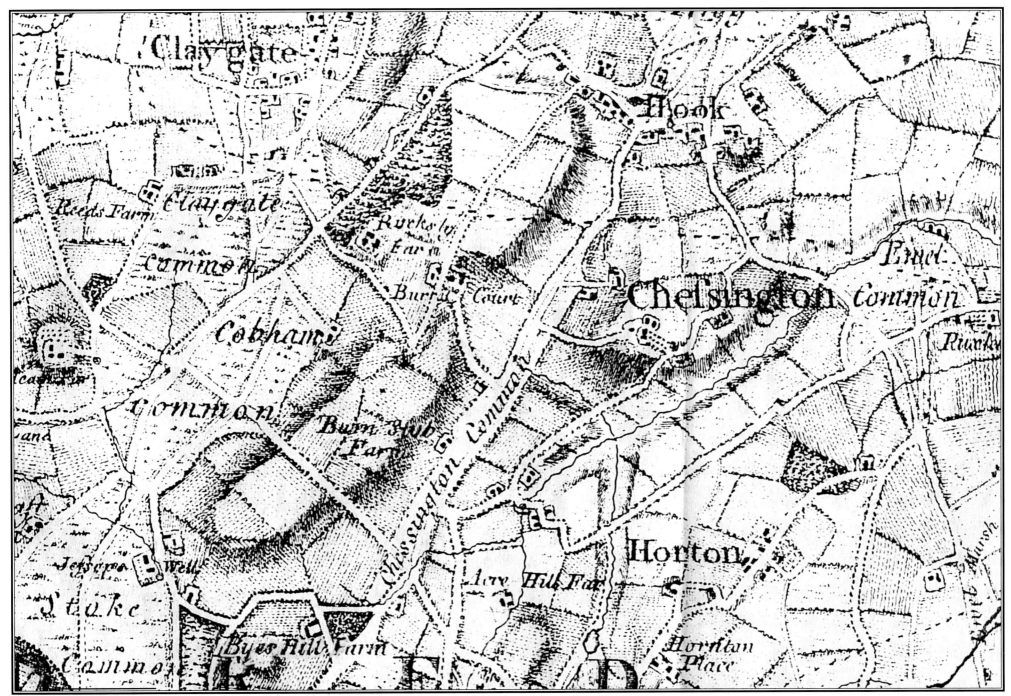

Chessington in 1768 consisted of a few farms and the church. Acre Hill Farm, 'Burn' Stub and 'Byes Hill' Farm are shown.

A deep, dark and damp forest hostile to visits from man

'Cissendune's' early villagers and a Roman tile factory in the woods

ANCIENTLY, Chessington was covered in dense forests and the first settlers probably entered this dark and damp habitat by following the course of the Hogsmill and its tributaries leading off the River Thames near Kingston.

Research carried out in the 1970s by Mr D J Field, of Mount Road, Chessington, provides many clues to how this inhospitable forest came to be inhabited.

Mr Field believed that thousands of years ago, these waterways were probably deeper than they are today. A few flint tools have been found and in 1998, using metal detectors, four fine Iron Age gold coins were unearthed by off-duty policemen at a secret farmland location in Malden Rushett. A further coin has since been discovered by the two men and the finds have been purchased by Kingston Museum.

On the heavy clay soil, away from the higher parts of the area, the oak woods grew densely and would have been the home of wild boar, bears, wolves and millions of midges and mosquitoes.

The Hogsmill crosses Chessington lengthways. Evidence of man's activities has been found in the form of flints dating back to the Mesolithic period, about 7,000 years ago, at Ewell and Malden.

During the Bronze and Iron Ages, settlements were established at Kingston, and about this time at Ashtead Woods, close to Malden Rushett, and at Malden. Mr Field presumes that a track would have linked the Ashtead and Malden settlements.

Part of the track is thought to have been along Green Lane, Chessington. A 1620 map by Charles Good shows a mile-long hedgerow and path: "This waye goes from Rushett to Malden." There is a fork in this road. One route goes to Ashtead, the other to Leatherhead. At the north end of the parish, the lane passes close to Castle Hill.

"The camp on Ashtead Common, just a few hundred yards south of the Chessington boundary, consists of a substantial, diamond-shaped earthworks enclosure that probably enclosed a few huts. Flint tools found in the vicinity point to it being occupied in either the Bronze or Iron Age," wrote Mr Field.

"The fields attached to this community must at one time have covered a large part of Chessington. A sherd of pottery was also found in the 1970s near Barwell Court.

"In Roman times, on Ashtead Common, a substantial villa was built and close to it, a tile factory. The factory, *(in woods just yards behind Rushett Farm)* which probably produced much of the roofing for the Roman houses at Ewell, had a long and prosperous life. First built about the year 80AD, it continued in operation well into the middle of the second century. It flourished particularly towards the end of that period, for its products were then being traded far and wide in England. Tiles from the kilns have been found as far afield as Staffordshire, Lincolnshire and the Mendip regions.

"Obviously, it must have brought a great amount of wealth to the region as well as providing work for local craftsmen. But primarily, the villa's main interest must have been in farming. South East England was renowned during the Celtic and Roman periods for its grain production."

The workers most likely lived in small round huts made from wattle and daub, with thatched roofs.

Only the most determined early farmers would have hunted and farmed in what became Chessington since the land was so marshy and impenetrable.

There is evidence of a settlement at Barwell Court Farm and it is likely that this was under the old farmhouse itself.

An early historian wrote that a large, brass Roman coin was unearthed near Castle Hill, and Roman pottery at Barwell.

Two other Roman coins have been discovered – both of them at Moor Lane School. A Roman settlement in Chessington cannot be determined – just evidence of visits at this stage.

In Saxon times, the thick forest continued to thrive and settlements centred on "Maeldune" – the hill with the cross – which is now Malden.

"Families continued to explore along the Hogsmill and its tributaries, exploring the countryside around as they did so. A mile beyond Maeldune, a Saxon called Tula decided to settle with his family. The resulting community became known as Tula's Weard (Tolworth).

It is assumed Saxons settled in the valley at the foot of Church Lane, Chessington, rather than at Ewell, where the British were living in the former Roman-occupied village.

Other explorers moved on deeper into the forest to the Rushett area of Chessington.

"About a mile to the south of the first farmstead near Church Lane, a second settlement became established on the other side of the hill. This hill may have had at one time a thin layer of gravel capping it. This seems to have prompted the Saxons to call the area *Cisendune,* meaning gravelly hill."

The Saxons probably cut down many trees and used the timber to build homes. Three fields in Chessington were cultivated. They were Down Field, which stretched northwards towards Tolworth; South Field, to the east, which extended down towards the stream; and Moor Field, to the west of the village, which extended to near Hook. Wheat, rye, barley, oats, peas, or spring barley were the likely crops to have been grown.

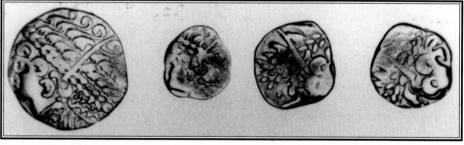

These four gold Iron age coins (not to scale), were unearthed on a Malden Rushett farm by policemen Andrew Dunn and Gary Row. The treasure trove has been purchased by Kingston Museum.

Harvest-time in the fields at Chessington in about 1890. The photograph was taken by John Tims, of Chessington Road, who toured the district on a penny farthing bicycle, capturing on camera some of these delightful rural scenes.

Chessington's timber used for Hampton Court and Nonsuch Palace

MUCH of the land in Chessington has been owned by Merton College, Oxford, for hundreds of years. In the 12th century, a former Surrey sheriff, Gilbert the Knight, founded a monastery in the area and funded a new order which had been introduced from the continent. The black-robed Augustinian canons were based at Merton Priory and had the blessing of King Henry I who granted Merton Priory a royal charter in 1121.

The priory developed strong links with Kingston Parish Church. In 1158, Henry II granted Merton Priory the manor Ewell.

Local land deals in the 12th century included the leasing by the "men of Surbeton" of a strip of land called Grapelingeham, near Barwell Court, to the Merton canons. This piece of land was later known as The Grapsom and archaeologists dug up the area in the 1970s and found evidence of a medieval farm before the whole site was covered in concrete for the building of the Esher by-pass.

Today, Merton College is still the greatest landowner in Chessington.

After the period of the dissolution of the monasteries in about 1535, there was considerable activity in the area, particularly at Malden Rushett. A road was cut through the woods from Oxshott to Epsom so that felled timber from Chessington's Great Oaks Wood, Sixty Acre Wood and the Crown woodland could be transported to Hampton Court Palace and Nonsuch Palace. Large quantities of timber from Great Oaks were used for the construction of Nonsuch Palace in the 1500s by King Henry VIII. The king had enclosed the Chessington woods as crown land in order to provide himself with a good hunting ground near Hampton Court.

How Chessington Church looked in about 1823 when C T Cracklow made this sketch to accompany a heavyweight book about the history of Surrey. Inset: The church c1800.

Queen bought up land

CARTLOADS of timber were transported from Chessington to Cheam for the building of Nonsuch Palace along a track which later became known as Rushett Lane and Fairoak Lane.

During construction in the 16th century, the Earl of Arundel bought Nonsuch Palace for £468. However, Queen Elizabeth I was also attracted to the building and probably one of its residents, and she had her heart set on buying it.

In a bid to persuade the Earl of Arundel to sell it to her, she offered him the crown land at Chessington after she negotiated a deal with Merton Priory for a 5,000-year lease.

The Earl of Arundel accepted, but later the queen's interest in Nonsuch diminished and after major arguments between Merton Priory and all parties, the woodland reverted to the Priory's ownership, initially on an 80-year lease and in 1707 on a permanent basis.

In the Stuart period during the 1600s, civil war broke out and rumours have always abounded that in the conflict between supporters of Charles I – the Royalists – and the Roundheads fighting for Parliament and Oliver Cromwell – that a large mansion called Burnt Stub was burned down.

This theory has been ruled out by local historians including Mark Barker whose family owned Chessington Hall and later Barwell Court.

Burnt Stub, claimed Mr Barker, was a humble tavern in the 1670s kept by a Mr Best who on one occasion was "hauled up" by the local authorities for conducting "loose affairs" at the beerhouse. This probably, Mr Barker said, would have concerned activities such as allowing people to get drunk and permitting the playing of cards on a Sunday when people should have been in church. Mr Best was fined for his bad behaviour.

There was a battle, however, on Kingston Common during the Civil War in which the Duke of Buckingham was shot dead.

In 1662, the main Kingston to Leatherhead road, then known as Hoke Lane, was falling into bad repair, and a call was made for the residents of Chessington to dig deep into their pockets to find the money for its improvement. A report said that "Hoke Lane cannot be passed without great danger". The following year, Chessington villagers were twice told by the powers-that-be to find the cash.

Meanwhile, at Malden Rushett, Thomas Lucas was fined for allowing Russett Ditch on Chessington Common to overflow, causing an inconvenience to people living in the vicinity.

The original Bonesgate public house stood very close to the Hogsmill tributary at the end of Moor Lane. The pub was known as The Gate at the end of the 1700s. Landlord Borne's gate, by a footbridge he built over the watersplash, was open only during his pub hours.

The men of Chessington used to put on shows at Chessington School, Leatherhead Road, in the early part of the 20th century. Among those in the group is Nibby 'Nibbs' Saker, Frank Styles and Ernest Partridge. Ernest lived on the corner of Almshouse Lane and Leatherhead Road, just yards from the old school which was demolished in the 1970s when a new school was opened near the church.

Mr and Mrs Tozer (above) ran Chessington School, Leatherhead Road, in the 1890s when John Tims took this picture.

Meadows and fields swept down from Chessington Church when this photograph was taken by John Tims in about 1890.

Rolling cornfields of rural Chessington

CHESSINGTON in the 1800s was just a scattered hamlet of a few dozen farm cottages, a church, school and a few mansions surrounded by fields and muddy lanes.

By 1850, the sleepy little village was shaken from its slumbers by the "redoubtable" vicar, Rev Chetwynd Stapylton. Local historian Mark Barker once said that Mr Stapylton "really was the founder of what happened in Chessington" and soon enthusias-tically reorganised the church.

"Before he arrived, the inside of the church was like Hampton Court maze when trying to get to the front for there were so many pews. He appealed for £600 and rebuilt the church in its present form and constructed a second aisle," said Mr Barker.

The reopening of the new-look church was in 1854 – the year of the first edition of the *Surrey Comet* – although full coverage of the ceremony was covered at that time by the established *Sussex Chronicle* newspaper. The journal told how "many carriages wended their way to the church in the glorious country-side". No doubt they travelled on the Kingston to Leatherhead turnpike road built after an act of Parliament was passed in 1811. Tolls had to be paid outside The Maypole, Hook Road, for the upkeep of the road that had cost £930 13s 4d to build.

Strange tale of a recluse

Hermit's life

IN the 1850s, a young woman who had been in domestic service came home to her mother's isolated Chessington cottage "in miserable health".

Her mother, a Mrs Shrub, lived off the very muddy Epsom Lane – now Rushett Lane – by Glanmire Farm.

One day, the vicar of Malden, the Rev Chetwynd Stapylton, called at the solitary cottage, a short walk from Epsom Common, and took pity on the girl.

In his diaries, the clergyman wrote: "Although I had several doctors to see her, none could do any good.

"There she remained for 20 years, mostly in bed. She grew worse and worse. I went constantly to see her and found her a most interesting case. Unable to read or write, I was able to teach her to do both perfectly.

"She lived a solitary life with her mother and no one else. She was a remarkable and exceptional person. She heard nothing, nor cared for anything that happened beyond her own cottage. She lived the life of a hermit.

"Her mother was by no means kind to her, but harsh. Not after many years she was overcome by her daughter's wonderful faith and patience and became a changed and converted woman.

"One day while walking in the garden, the daughter fell into a deep pond and drowned. Her mother at last felt relief that it was all over."

Church Lane, Chessington, in 1889 was just a narrow country road leading up to the parish church. Here, two gents exchange village news over the garden fence in front of one of the old cottages at the foot of the lane. This photograph was taken by John Tims.

Two villagers in Church Lane stop for a chat near the church in 1889.

Woman, 97, attacked at cottage

DIARIES kept by a Chessington vicar during his 44 years' work in the village between 1850 and 1894 give reference to some curious old characters.

One of them, 97-year-old Sarah "Old Dame" Townsend appears to have been attacked in her home by a home-help during a violent quarrel.

Rev Chetwynd Stapylton wrote in his daily notes that "Old Dame" Townsend was a "quaint, sprightly, old woman, who, even at the age of 90, was known to have walked as far as Epsom to take a job as a sick nurse or midwife.

"She would would wear a scarlet cloak and a black satin coal shuttle bonnet."

Some years previously, he said, she had lived down the lane from the church in a thatched cottage. One day, the thatch caught fire and the cottage burnt down.

Out of the thatch fell a number of sovereigns wrapped up in stockings, which, according to Mr Stapylton's informant, were largely appropriated by her sons.

Homeless, she moved to Glebe Cottage, opposite the church. This old cottage of just four rooms had a large shrubbery at the back and a barn. As early as the 1850s, the old men of Chessington were describing it as being well over 200 years old.

Although active, "Old Dame" Townsend was getting on in years "and at the ripe old age of 97 she had a young girl living with her to help her out with several physical tasks."

One day, the pair of them had an argument and the girl gave "Old Dame" Townsend a push.

The old lady fell and hit her head on the fireplace. The girl, frightened, panicked and ran several miles to her home.

Later in the day, a passing tramp found old Sarah laying as she fell, with her head still in the grate. She was completely paralysed.

Doctors were called but they could do nothing and she died shortly afterwards.

On her wooden grave were carved the words: "The physicians' toil was all in vain, her precious life they could not save".

Glebe Cottage was afterwards improved by Mr Stapylton and was used by the curates of the parish.

The two timber cottages in the photograph on the left have now disappeared. Built on the site in 1897 were four homes, called Frearn Cottages, after the original name of one of the Chessington manors, whose manor house was Chessington Hall.

Frearn Cottages were still standing more than 100 years later, in millennium year, but were numbered 127-133 Church Lane.

Two other cottages over the road, and a little further away from the church were Newdigate Cottage and Homeside Cottage, also built in 1897, the year of Queen Victoria's diamond jubilee.

The old Fox and Hounds

A cart from the Epsom corn and coal merchant's has pulled up outside the old Fox and Hounds public house in Leatherhead Road, Chessington, in about 1905. This beerhouse was pulled down in the early 1930s and rebuilt. The new public house, in modern times, provides a useful refreshment stop for motorists turning off the M25 after a long journey, or those visiting the World of Adventures half a mile up the road. As a girl in the early 1930s, Ann Whetstone stayed with relatives in one of the wooden cottages next to the beerhouse when her mother contracted a fever and was unable to look after her. "There was no water laid on and I remember getting water from a stopcock half way up the garden. Also, there were no stairs. The building was just two up and two down. A fixed ladder was used to get to the upper floor and I remember we would kneel at the top to say our prayers to grandad and step grandmother who would listen to us from the foot of the ladder. At night, my gran used to plait my hair and tie it in rags for me to go to bed."

A gaggle of geese waddle around the grassy roadside in Moor Lane, near the Bonesgate, in 1889. Moor Lane was an ancient road linking Ewell and Hook.

Chessington in 1855

CHESSINGTON Church was accessible only by footpaths and lanes in 1855. The churchyard outside the newly-refurbished church "commanded picturesque views of Epsom and Ewell, while the hall adjoining (Chessington Hall), now the classic residence of George Chancellor, Esq, a further prospect is obtained of the neighbourhood of Leatherhead, Esher, and Kingston," according to a contemporary guidebook.

The new-look church was opened by Reverend W C Staplyton MA on Thursday 20th April 1854.

The population of Chessington was just 229 people in 1851 and the parish covered 1,229 acres.

Among the listed gentry living in the village were farmer George Bird; George Chancellor; Reverend George Bridges Lewis, the curate; Thomas Wallis, at Chessington Lodge (Burnt Stub); farmers George Cobbett, William Hardwick, John Humphrey (Copt Gilders Hall) and Joseph Merrick; Thomas Robinson, a wheelwright, and Samuel Townsend, who ran the Harrow Inn, Leatherhead Road.

Mail was received at Kingston for Chessington and the nearest money order office was at Epsom.

This little hamlet was incredibly only 15 miles from central London.

The Barker family

THE name Barker is synonymous with Chessington for this notable family had links with the village throughout the 20th century.

Sir Francis Barker lived at Burnt Stub, which he had built between 1906 and 1911 in mock Jacobean style on the site of an old beerhouse and farm. He gave land for a recreation ground in Leatherhead Road which was named after him and also relaunched the thriving Chessington Cricket Club in 1919.

He was the second son of Alfred Barker, of Elmfield, Esher, and died in January 1922 at the age of 57. His father was a banker in Constantinople and it was there he was born. He began, in his father's bank, a business career that was to take him around the world and lead him to become one of the foremost international traders of the period. He was noted for building up strong trading links with Russia.

His connections led him to help Russian refugees and it was for this reason that a Russian prince, Vladimir Galitzine, came to live at Chessington Hall with his princess wife for several years up to 1936 when the Barker family moved in.

Sir Francis and his wife, Lady Aimee Barker, who later lived at Barwell Court and was a great benefactor to the area, had two sons, Arthur, a publisher, and Vere. Arthur had three sons, Tim, Mark, and Patrick. Mark had two sons, Hugo and Simon, and a daughter, Annabelle. Tim had two children by

Sir Francis Barker – built Burnt Stub mansion between 1906 and 1911.

his first wife and two by his second.

Some of the family moved away, but Mark Barker and his wife stayed in Chessington, residing for many years at Virginia Cottage, Barwell Court.

Mark followed in his grandfather's footsteps when he attempted to set up strong sporting links between England and the Soviet Union.

As a boy, Mark recalls watching from the roof of Chessington Hall, in his pyjamas, the glow in the sky from the great fire at Crystal Palace in 1936.

For some years, the Barker family lived in White Oaks, Garrison Lane, which Arthur built in 1929, Lady Barker laying the foundation stone.

Mark recalled: "It cost less than £400 to build. It was a lovely house with parquet floors."

Mrs Ford's refreshment stall in the garden of a little cottage opposite the Bonesgate public house in Moor Lane.

Mrs Ford's refreshment stall – and 'Porky' White

IN THE early 1900s, cyclists, villagers and passers-by used to stop for lemonade or ginger beer at a refreshment stall outside Mrs Mary Ford's cottage opposite the Bonesgate public house.

The tea stall was run by Mrs Ford, whose daughter, Annie, born in 1884, rented the cottage for 5s (25p) a week.

While Mrs Ford ran the little tea garden, Annie worked as a market gardener, starting work at 3.30am and getting paid 2d (1p) a punnet in the strawberry season. Her daily wage for general market gardening work was 1s 6d (7p). Sometimes she would pick blackberries from the hedgerows and take them to Kingston jam factory, pushing them eight miles there and back in an old pram.

During the 1914 war, Annie met her husband, a Scot named Muir, who was serving with the Australian forces. She was carrying out war work at a Surrey hospital. They married in Scotland and emigrated to Australia. There they lived poorly, but in 1956 won an Australian lottery and with the £500 proceeds, arranged a trip back to England, revisiting Chessington.

In later years, "Porky" White, son of a butcher from Epsom's indoor market, and a property owner, made memorably tasty sausages from a butcher's premises uphill from the Bonesgate. This short, chubby character died and a "Porky" White trophy in his memory is awarded annually at Leatherhead Golf Course.

The Bonesgate beerhouse, Moor Lane, where there was an argument over a closed gate.

This gate hangs high and hinders none . . .

THE strangely-named Bonesgate public house has intrigued locals and passers-by for many years. Rumours have abounded that a pit of bones from a medieval plague could be found nearby.

But the more obvious explanation is that the title is derived from a landlord of the alehouse. The picture above shows the earlier building of the same name as the present public house. It stood closer to the little stream, a tributary of the Hogsmill, than the current premises.

Up until the end of the 18th century, the beerhouse was known simply as The Gate. A landlord of that the time, a Mr Borne, apparently built a footbridge over the watersplash, only opening it during trading but an outraged public demanded that he removed the gate.

With a rare sense of humour, he hung up the gate from a willow tree and on it painted the words: "This gate hangs high and hinders none, refresh and pay and travel on."

A later misspelling of Borne's name as Bone gave the place its name of the Bone's Gate. The tributary has also become known as the Bonesgate stream.

In Australia, there is a possible link with the Bonesgate. At Greengate, in Killara, near Sydney, there is a similar sign, bearing identical wording. It is thought it may be the work of an early immigrant from Chessington.

Water from a well

TIZER and lemonade were 2d (1p) a bottle at Mrs Ford's refreshment stall in 1926 when Reg Driver was a boy.

On approaching his 80th birthday, Reg looked back fondly on his childhood days which took him daily past the Bonesgate watersplash.

"I used to run through the watersplash on the way home from school but not on the way to school because I would get my feet wet," he said.

Mrs Ford, who sold refreshments.

"Often after school we were thirsty in summer. There were two little shops – Ford's and one on the opposite side of the road, Mr Chatfield's, in one of the two cottages.

"There, you could get water out of a well and they would wind the bucket up for you. They would give you an enamel cup and you could have a drink."

Reg was living at Scott's Farm, Ruxley Lane, West Ewell, from 1925 to 1927 and made daily trips on foot to St Paul's School, Hook.

He helped his farmhand father, Fred Driver, on many occasions, sometimes carrying the milk across the road in two buckets. The Driver family lived in one of a pair of cottages opposite the Kingfisher public house.

Reg knew Mrs Ford as "Mrs Batey" because of the Batey soft drinks advertisements outside her home in the dip by the Bonesgate.

"The little old lady at the shop was the nicest person you'd ever seen," he recalled.

Reg's mother would regularly trudge past the Bonesgate with heavy bags of shopping she had lugged several miles.

Mrs Ford came to Chessington having previously lived with her family in Kingston and in Minniedale, Surbiton. Her daughter, Annie, had rented the cottage opposite the Bonesgate, as a young woman.

The watersplash outside the Bonesgate public house, Chessington, in late Victorian times.

A mother and her children take a stroll in 1889 to Steeple Pond, Chessington. Contemporary maps do not show a pond by this name. There was a 30ft wide pond at the junction of Church Lane and Moor Lane but this view is thought to show another at the fork in two paths – one which led to Copt Gilders Hall and another, wider, track to the steepled Chessington Church. Before dividing into two, the path led from Chessington Road, West Ewell, across Butcher's Grove, across a field to the Bonesgate stream and then up to the forked junction. The photograph was taken by John Tims.

'The Chessington country'

FOR those who wished to escape the hustle and bustle of London life at weekends the bus and train companies published a book in 1924 giving details of beauty spots a short distance from the capital.

One chapter in the interesting little publication is devoted to "The Chessington Country". The author describes an idyllic place for lovers of nature and fresh air.

"After crossing the railway line at Surbiton, a straight and open road runs through Hook and Chessington, reaching Leatherhead in some six-and-a-half miles.

"Hook is a suburban district, but nothing could be more rustic than the fields about the small Church of Chessington, a short distance to the East of the main road.

"The road between Hook and Leatherhead is singularly beautiful. It is the country of nature-writer Richard Jefferies, author of Nature Near London.

"The daily service of motor buses to Hook is most convenient for this Chessington countryside, for Claygate, Telegraph Hill, Ashtead Woods, for cornfields, woods, meadows every country delight; such meadows as we find hereabouts, in their frames of hawthorn hedges, can hardly be found in any other part of the country so near London.

"And this countryside is remarkable for its wild flowers, and for the germander speedwells which cover every bank in May.

"Chessington Hall, near the church, is associated with Fanny Burney, who here visited Samuel Crisp, dancing around the mulberry tree on learning, as a girl, that her book, "Evelina", had made her famous. The tree still stands in the grounds of the hall, and is seen from the bridle road to the church.

"In the church is a tablet to the memory of Crisp (died 1783), with an epitaph written by Dr C Burney, telling how his wisdom and wit 'chear'd and enlighten'd all this hamlet round'.

"The church has fine timbering; a 16th century iron chest; and fragments of 15th century alabaster carvings: one is preserved by the altar in a frame."

The book also perpetuates rumours that Cromwell's men caused destruction in the neighbourhood. "They found their way to this remote church and wrought havoc."

The wide view of Epsom from the churchyard is praised and "a footpath runs to Epsom, offering a charming walk in summer. There is also a footpath to Hook."

The main (Leatherhead) road "has wide, grassy borders, and runs through a sparsely populated and pleasant countryside, passing by woods and commons, with Ashtead Common on the left, open country after a rambler's heart."

Chessington-at-Hoke, Fream, Copp Guilders

The Chessington manors

AFTER the Norman Conquest in the 11th century, Richard de Tonbridge, a Norman baron, who came to England with the Conqueror, received extensive lands in England. Among the 38 manors in Surrey which he received were Malden and Chessington. Since then, until more modern times, Malden and Chessington were closely linked. This explains the name Malden Rushett.

One of the first mentions of Chessington Church is in the Merton Priory records, dated 1174-1189, when Richard, Bishop of Winchester, confirmed to the Priory the advowson of "the Church of Meldona and the Chapel of Chissendon".

By 1249, the manors of Malden and Chessington had been granted to Walter de Merton, and in 1262 a licence was granted for the presentation of the manors to the House of Scholars which Walter de Merton was founding at Malden.

Later, in 1264, Walter de Merton assigned the manors by charter to this house for the support of 20 scholars by then at Oxford.

So, the manors became part of Merton College, Oxford, – the estate at Chessington later becoming known as Chessington Park. After this, Merton Priory put Malden Church and Chessington Chapel under Walter de Merton and the House of Scholars at Oxford. The college still retains much land at Chessington and Malden Rushett.

In 1578, the college passed the lands to the Earl of Arundel only to retrieve them in 1707.

The link with Malden carried on until 1938, even though as early as 1648 attempts had been made to hive it off because wet and muddy lanes between the two communities made it so impractical to work together. "Chissington lyeth distant from Mauldon about two miles" and "the waies between this and Mauldon" were "extreame foule and impassable in the winter season," old church documents tell us.

Separation was apparently made briefly at one stage and for a time, "Chissington" supposedly had its own curate, but it soon reverted to coming under Malden again. The separation, some believe, only referred to civil boundaries, not those of the church parishes.

Another estate in Chessington, probably the original manor, was acquired by Merton Priory and is mentioned in 16th century monastic accounts as "the manor of Chessington-at-Hoke".

In the 1530s, when the monasteries were dissolved under Henry VIII, the manor plus other Priory assetts passed to the Crown. In 1553, some of the church treasures, including water cruets of lead, banner clothes, towels of linen, a red satin cloak, brass items and a silver chalice, were sold to raise money to repair "More" Lane, to wash the church and pay for court fees. The sum raised was 7s (35p).

During the early years of Queen Elizabeth I, the church acquired a silver communion cup which was later presented to the Victoria and Albert Museum. It is dated 1568.

Other land in Chessington seems to have been held by the Abbot of Boxley in Kent, probably since the 12th century, though the land was not described as a manor until 1535 when it was included among the monastic lands under the name of 'the manor of Frier'. This land, too, was surrendered to the Crown on the dissolution of the monasteries.

The manors subsequently changed hands and were held in the late 1700s by Sir Robert Hatton, Recorder of Kingston, who died in 1682. He was succeeded by his nephew Robert, who later settled the manors on his son, Thomas Hatton. The manor of Chessington was sold by Thomas Hatton, though he kept the manor of Friern, later known as Fream, until his death in 1746.

Fream was then bought by Christopher Hamilton, with whom lived Samuel Crisp *(see pages 20 and 21)*.

Hamilton was succeeded by his sister. When she died, Fream, or by then Chessington Hall, changed hands again. In 1839, it was held by Rev Henry Penny, and in 1851 was bought by Horatio Chancellor. The house, said to have dated from 1520, had become ruinous and was rebuilt in 1833-34. Chessington Hall was pulled down and a council housing estate towards the top of Garrison Lane was built on its land after the Second World War.

In 1797, the manor of Chessington-at-Hoke was bought by Joseph Smith Gosse, a distiller, of Battersea, who died in 1812. He was succeeded by his son, Henry Gosse, and the family held the land into recent times. In the 1730s, there is mention of Copp Guilders Hall, later Copt Gilders, and Henry Gosse is mentioned in connection with Copt Gilders Hall Farm in 1853.

In 1821, the population of Chessington was just 150 people. The little church was to be given a boost when the visionary Rev Chetwynd Staplyton, born 1825, and educated at Eton, arrived in 1850 as vicar of Malden and Chessington and stayed until he retired in 1894, having achieved much.

Wheelwrights and funeral directors

Kelsey's forge

Jack Kelsey (inset) and his workshop.

FOR more than a century, the Kelsey family has been linked with Chessington. Tom Kelsey came over from Ireland in the 1880s and for a time, he and his wife, Mary, taught at schools in the parish. They had three children. One of them, Jack, ran the forge, wheelwright's, builder's and undertaker's in Leatherhead Road, opposite the Harrow pub which had previously been a small stagecoach inn catering for horses on one of the London to Brighton routes. The new Harrow was rebuilt by Jack Kelsey around the turn of the last century.

Older Chessington residents recall coffins propped up outside the forge in bygone times.

Jack was heavily involved in building Chessington Zoo in the early 1930s. He employed six bricklayers and six carpenters and legend has it that the zoo was ready for opening six weeks after the land had been bought by Reginald Goddard in 1931.

After the war, when motor transport became the norm, the forge shut and Jack Kelsey worked for the Ministry for Admiralty, transporting cork to this country to construct lifeboats.

Jack married a girl called Charlotte – known as Effie – who hailed from Claygate. Jack's son, Raymond, was still living next door to the forge site in 1999, maintaining the long family link with Chessington.

The forge and cottage.

Fanny Burney and an eccentric recluse

Chessington Hall

THERE is no place where I more really enjoy myself than at Chessington. These words were written in 1777 by authoress Fanny Burney, who spent long periods of time at Chessington Hall.

Fanny Burney was one of the famous celebrities of the 18th and 19th century. She spent many happy hours at the isolated 16th century hall kept by family friend Samuel Crisp.

Mr Crisp was a rather eccentric London playwright who enjoyed only a limited success with his works. Rather disillusioned with City life and wishing to retire from the limelight and its pitfalls, he moved out into the countryside to the remote hamlet of Chessington.

His rambling property, once named Frearn House, was the perfect place for young Fanny to work on her books, which are still in print today.

Indeed, it is recorded that on learning about the success of her first novel, Evelina, she danced merrily around the mulberry tree in the garden of Chessington Hall.

Fanny first met Samuel Crisp in 1764 and wrote that he was her "earliest and dearest friend." He became her mentor and inspiration and a substitute parent. Often she referred to him as Daddy Crisp.

At Chessington Hall she could flee the burdensome duties at home and carry on with her writing. Mr Crisp gave her a room at Chessington Hall which he called "the conjuring closet".

Fanny wrote of the hall: "All the household are kind, hospitable, and partial to me. There is no sort of restraint – everybody is disengaged and at liberty to pursue their own inclinations – and my Daddy, who is the soul of the place, is at once so flatteringly affectionate to me, and so infinitely, so beyond comparison in himself, that were I to be otherwise than happy in his company, I must either be wholly without feeling or utterly destitute of understanding."

Fanny kept her writing secret from her family and it was because of Mr Crisp's encouragement that Evelina was published anonymously.

Straightaway it was a best-seller and on learning that it had been praised by Dr Johnson, she hurried gleefully into the garden and performed her now-famous dance

An early sketch of the 16th century Chessington Hall, where Samuel Crisp was in residence and where Fanny Burney celebrated the success of her first novel, Evelina, by dancing around the mulberry tree.

around the mulberry tree.

In 1793, at the age of 40, she married a poor French Royalist refugee, General Alexandre D'Arblay, who had lost his properties in France.

In 1801, he returned to France and Fanny was in Paris as Napoleon marched against England and in Brussels when Wellington's epic victory at Waterloo made history. She vividly chronicled these events in her well-known diaries.

She gave birth to her first child aged 42 and at the age of 60 had a cancerous breast removed without an anaesthetic. She lived another 29 years without the illness returning.

To people in Chessington, her time spent at the hall is the most interesting aspect of her life. But it is worth mentioning some of Miss Burney's other colourful periods. For five years she was second keeper of the robes to Queen Charlotte, wife of George III, and was privileged to know intimate secrets of the royal family between 1786 and 1791. She saw that the king and queen and

their 13 children lived a domestic life much like any other family, with much affection between husband and wife. Fanny spent summers at Kew Palace with the king and queen who appeared most relaxed here.

Fanny was at court when the king's illness overwhelmed him. It had erroneously been diagnosed as madness, and in her journals she had written of the heartbreak it caused. At the illness's peak, Fanny was the queen's main confidante.

Fanny's true father, Dr Charles Burney, was one of the country's finest music teachers and historians of the time. Through him she met Dr Johnson, the diarist, and David Garrick, the actor.

Later in her life, she met Sir Walter Scott, who was apparently much influenced by her novels. Fanny wrote four novels between 1778 and 1814. They were Evelina, Cecilia, Camilla and The Wanderer. Her plays and some of her diaries are in print today. She died in 1840, having outlived her husband and son.

Fanny Burney as painted by her cousin, Edward Francesco Burney. Fanny's happiest times were at Chessington.

Samuel Crisp teased

SAMUEL Crisp had no idea that Fanny Burney had written Evelina, even though he had warmly encouraged her to keep diaries. Mischievous Fanny had wound him up over the true authorship of the book until the secret could no longer be concealed.

The teasing continued during a visit by Fanny's father to the hall. Her father had been singing the praises of the book and its characters. Samuel Crisp had said it was a "wonderful" novel but neither knew Fanny had penned it.

Fanny recalled in her diaries that an hour later, "... as I was passing through the hall, I met daddy (Crisp). His face was all animation and archness. He doubled his fist at me, and would have stopped me, but I ran past him into the parlour.

"Before supper, however, I again met him and he would not suffer me to escape; he caught both my hands and looked as if he would have looked me through and then exclaimed, "Why, you little hussy – you young devil! – aren't you ashamed to look me in the face, you *Evelina* you! Why, what a dance have you led me about it! Young friend indeed! O you little hussy, what tricks have you served me!"

The hall had 23 rooms plus a beer cellar, stables, a coach house, brewhouse, pigeon house and apple chamber.

Samuel Crisp died in 1783 and was buried in Chessington Church and his life is commemorated by an engraved memorial tablet on the north-west wall of the church.

After Crisp's death, Chessington Hall was leased to a Colonel Dalrymple, aide-de-camp to the future William IV, who let him use it for for his assignations with the actress Mrs Jordan.

The 16th century hall was pulled down and rebuilt in 1833.

In 1946, the Barker family were forced to sell it to Surbiton Borough Council under a compulsory purchase order and 400 council homes were built in the house's grounds at the top of Garrison Lane. The old house survived until 1965 when it was demolished and eight

Samuel Crisp, the former London playwright, who retired to the tranquillity of Chessington Hall.

homes were built on the site.

The only local memorial to Fanny Burney is a block of flats on the Chessington Hall estate, off the Leatherhead Road. These flats are named Evelina House, Camilla House, Burney House and Cecilia House.

The Burney Avenue in Surbiton recalls her great nephew, Archdeacon Charles Burney, who was vicar of St Mark's Church, Surbiton Hill, for three-and-a-half decades until his death in 1907.

The avenue which led from Leatherhead Road to Chessington Hall.

A late Victorian photo of the dovecote in Chessington Hall's 23 acres.

The avenue to Chessington Hall

THIS avenue led off the Leatherhead Road to Chessington Hall – or Chancellor's Farm – as it was known when this photograph was taken by John Tims in about 1890. Today, the track has gone and has long-since been replaced by the tarmacadamed Garrison Lane. In the 18th century the lane was lined by Spanish chestnut trees.

"Garrison" comes from "Garson", – "gaerstun", old English for grassy enclosure. There were two arable fields Lower Garson and Upper Goorston on a 1796 map.

In the 18th century, authoress Fanny Burney described Chessington Hall as being a house of nooks and corners with "quarters of staircases" leading to unused rooms.

She wrote of "garrets, or rather cells in great number and in all shapes, to fit the capricious forms of the leaded roof; windows in angles nigh the ceiling; carven cupboards and carven chimney-pieces, above blue and white tiles."

There was also a tall, canopied bed, tied up to the ceiling, she said, and "Japan cabinets with two or three hundred drawers; old pictures and tapestry presenting knights and damosels." And before the windows, "straight old garden paths and across the leaden ridges of the roof a view of the country for 16 miles around."

Even though Samuel Crisp was 46 years her senior, "his affection made my sun shine", wrote Fanny.

Food supplies ran out

HILDA Mary Coppard was born at 2 Sunflower Cottages, Leatherhead Road, in 1915. So vivid were her delightful memories of those days in rural Chessington, she put pen to paper when retired so future generations could see just what a different world it was when she was a girl.

Hilda, who became Mrs Pratt when she married, was the second of eight children – seven of them boys. Her mother and father were Ada and Herbert Coppard.

"As I developed, I quickly learnt that the world was at war. Of course, I was too young to realise the seriousness of the situation, but my mother told me so much about what was going on, so I feel as if I have always known about it all. Life was difficult in those days. Everyone at home in the village was working hard for the war effort. Any man not in the services was found work in small munitions factories. Some took on the positions of special constables or volunteer nurses. Others worked on the farms or carried out various essential work.

"Many of the village folk were employed by the mental hospitals at Epsom, as attendants, nurses, works gardeners and the like. Some of this work carried on after the war.

"My dad was called up for service with the East Surrey Regiment and became a prisoner of war after an injury to his right arm. He was confined in Arras, France, before being sent to Germany.

"Food supplies began to run out and it meant a day's march to and from Epsom town to join the food queues. People stood patiently for hours to obtain bread, meat, sugar and margarine.

"My mother told me that the Government ordered

Heath Cottage, Sunflower, Wentworth and Myrtle Cottages about 1915.

Hilda Coppard and older brother Bert in 1922.

"war bread" to be made with wheaten flour. It was greyish brown in colour, dry and hard.

"I had to grow up quickly. I had to learn my mother's cooking and sewing skills and help look after my younger brothers. I had a very happy home life."

All the cottages in Chessington had coal ranges and the occupants were dependent on deliveries of coal and coke to keep the home fires burning. There was plenty of wood to be got from the woods, and in the village were two working wood yards. Mr Warren was the owner of one and Mr Whetstone the other. Both were in Leatherhead Road. I remember women being employed in the yards to do the splitting. They wore men's cloth caps and coarse hessian aprons for their protection. We were allowed into the sheds to pick up the "chips" for kindling. Each cottage had wooden planks forming a little bridge over a wide ditch to get on to the Leatherhead Road.

"Children were always falling in and the wheels of prams or trucks were always getting stuck between the planks. Life was generally good for the children.

"There was no gas, no electricity and no flush toilets in the village when I was a child. We came under Epsom Rural District Council *(until 1933)*. The council workmen came with their tools to keep the ditches clean and the grass verges tidy. There was no footpath so we had to walk along the Leatherhead Road. After the age of eight, we were considered too old to ride to school on Mr Whetstone's van so we used to run behind.

"Mr Whetstone never counted the number of children so many of them used to climb on the tailboard on the way along, and now and again some bully would shout, 'whip behind' and unless you were good at jumping, you felt a stinging crack across the legs. I well remember on hot sunny days on the long walk home, popping the tar bubbles and marvelling at the lovely colours of the rainbow that the odd drip of petrol made on the road."

Village's little shops

HILDA Coppard recalls that when she was a girl in the 1920s, there was a small shop in the village which took the form of a store in the front room of a private house. It was in Almond Tree Cottages by the brickworks run by Ebenezer Sayers in Leatherhead Road, near the present-day West Road.

"It sold small groceries, candles, paraffin and smelly red carbolic soap and sundry goods hanging on cards. I shall never forget the smell of the paraffin and soap. I sometimes used to go in there to buy a couple of candles – not much more – that's all you could afford. You could also buy stamps.

"Mrs Sayers, the shopkeeper, was a short, kind lady, rather plump with rosy cheeks." She was also the postmistress from 1926 to 1930.

"The brickworks next door was very busy and made flower pots, drain pipes, chimney pots, tiles and bricks. For races at school, they let us have all the cracked flower pots."

Hilda said a variety of tradesmen called at the village with their wares. A horse-drawn van from Pointer's at Hook delivered bread and groceries. Mr Chapman came round in a butcher's van which was sparkling white.

"He had his scales, chopping boards and large knives and did his cutting, weighing and selling from the van.

"So long as you had money there was food to be had. Everyone kept a kitchen garden and most folk had chickens and rabbits. Gypsy folk living on Epsom Common hawked clothes pegs, flowers made from wood shavings, wrap-over pinnies, knickers, vests, socks, stockings and haberdashery.

"I loved all the lace on the cards and the pretty coloured ribbons. I always had new ribbons after their visits.

"There were several working farms – Acre Hill Farm, Park Farm, Rushett Farm, Byhurst Farm and Rushett Dairy. Our milk came from Rushett Dairy. Deliveries were made twice a day from a cart with shiny measuring jugs hanging along the side. Mr Bailey, the dairyman, himself used to wheel the cart round. We could go to the dairy, watch the cows being milked and then see the milk put through the coolers and separators.

"We could buy skimmed milk for a halfpenny a jug, so we had lots of rice pudding, cooked all day in the slow oven of the coal range. It would be all nice and creamy.

"News would go round the village that Mr Sills or Mr

Leatherhead Road showing cottages on the south side of the Fox and Hounds in about 1908. In this row, the cottages include Hindhead, Haslemere, Shanklin, Ventnor and Walton.

Booker would be killing a pig. This would be an extra bonus for the family and orders for joints would be taken. There seemed to be no post office as such, although stamps could be bought in the sitting room of a Mrs Cole, next to the motor garage. She had a licence to sell tobacco and cigarettes and these could also be bought. She was a member of the Salvation Army and I remember her as an elderly woman with white hair.

"We went to St Mary the Virgin church on Sundays, away on the hill, and of course, had a long walk all the way there and back. There was a stile over the fields opposite Almshouse Lane and we could walk, keeping to the footpath, to the church.

"There was no Garrison Lane. We all knew it as Church Lane. There were wrought iron gates at the top and bottom of the lane, which were opened when access was required. The top ones took the form of a toll gate and next to these was Toll Gate Cottage where a charge was made for the gate to be opened to

let a carriage or funeral hearse through. There was a slip-gate for pedestrians.

"After the Russian revolution, Russian royalty took up residence at Chessington Hall. We had to pass the house on our way to church if we went along the lane or came up through the donkey field. We were so terrified of a Chinese servant who lived there, and of two vicious terrier dogs that flew at our legs if the gate was open. The mossy green banks in the lane were full of sweet-smelling white violets and primroses in the spring.

"St Mary's Church stands at the peak of the hill where Garrison Lane, Green Lane and Church Lane meet. The 12th century church has known the quiet obscurity of a rural scene but now sees the hustle and bustle of a fast-moving society.

"I was christened in 1915 at St Mary's by the curate of that time, William Charles Humbley, and confirmed in the days of Kenneth Otway Mayne in 1928."

The 'Iron Church'

LUSH green grass has always grown at the spot where the little Church of the Good Shepherd – also known as the Iron Church – once stood in Malden Rushett.

The tiny place of worship was opposite Star Cottages on the Leatherhead Road at Telegraph Hill, the highest point in the present Royal Borough of Kingston.

Here, villagers from the tiny hamlet of Malden Rushett – around the Star public house – and others from "over the hill" in Chessington, gathered on Sundays to pray and sing hymns.

As a girl, Hilda Coppard lived opposite the chapel, at Wood View, a few doors from The Star. She used to clean the church with help from three girls who lived near her home on the green.

In retirement, Hilda recalled:"It was the dear little Church of the Good Shepherd, built of corrugated iron with a matchboard interior. We understood it to be erected on non-consecrated ground, on land owned by Merton College.

"It was closed completely after the Second World War and removed afterwards. All services had ceased there when the Guildford Diocese took over and ties with Southwark were broken.

"In my childhood – just after the First World War – we had an 8am communion service once a month, and a 3pm evensong. Sometimes in the summer there would be an evening lecture. The morning service was conducted by the Rev Fynnes Clinton who came out from St John the Baptist, Old Malden, but the evening services were conducted by lay readers from Leatherhead, who included a Mr Burnett and a Mr Arnold, who brought with him his dear wife who played harmonium for us. There was a bell overhead which was rung by my brother, Victor Coppard, when he was aged 12.

"Lady Giller, the daughter of the Rev Chetwynd Staplyton, in charge of Malden and Chessington between 1850 and 1894, was a benefactor of this

Teenaged bellringer Victor Coppard outside the Iron Church, opposite the Star Cottages, Malden Rushett. In the first part of the 1900s, the locality name Malden Rushett was given only to the hamlet around The Star. Before 1884, the civil parish of Malden included the southern part of Chessington where addresses were given as "Malden, Surrey" or Malden Rushett, Leatherhead, Surrey" as far north as Rushett Dairy Farm. This was commonplace even several decades after Chessington became a separate civil parish. The locality name Malden Rushett was revived in the late 1970s and once again applies to an area from the Fairoak crossroads to the Star. Rushett probably means swampy land with rushes.

little church, which would seat about 60 people."

The congregation was made up of country folk including owners and workers on the nearby dairy farms.

"There was a small altar, candles, oil lamps and heating, a crucifix and a picture of 'Suffer The Little Children To Come Unto Me' by Margaret Tarrant. Pictures of 'The Stations of the Cross' adorned the walls," said Hilda.

A Mrs Jones and her friend, who lived next-door-but-one to the chapel at D'Abernon Lodge, were caretakers. The church was shaded by willows and fir trees.

At the age of 84, Hilda reminisced about the old church. "It was a sad day when it was closed down, as they could not get anyone to take the services. It is a strange thing that the grass grows lush and green where it stood."

Today, there is no visible evidence in the roadside thickets that a church ever stood at the site.

The village children of Chessington and Malden Rushett

A FASCINATING insight into the life of Chessington and Malden Rushett just after the 1914-18 war has been made possible by Hilda Pratt (nee Coppard).

In retirement at Durbin Road, Hook, Mrs Pratt wrote down a delightful collection of memories of those early days. And while in her 85th year, she decided to share them with others through this book.

Her story of homelife with no electricity, gas, or main drains, is told elsewhere. Remarkably, she was able to recall with great precision nearly all the names of the pupils at St Mary's School, Leatherhead Road, where she started her education at the age of five.

On the adjacent page is a group photograph showing some of the pupils at the little school in January 1923. Mrs Pratt had kept the picture for 75 years.

In the top row are seven boys. The first, looking from left to right, is Tom Mitchell, who lived in Church Lane, near St Mary's Church. The second is Bob Smithers, of Almond Tree Cottage, Leatherhead Road. The third boy has not been identified, but the fourth is George Smithers, who lived in the cottages just south of the Fox and Hounds.

Although the fifth boy's identity was uncertain, Mrs Pratt readily recalled the next boy in the line as being Bert Coppard, one of her seven brothers.

The pupil seventh from the left is Fred Day, whose family lived in a black, wooden cottage at the corner of Rushett Lane and Leatherhead Road, opposite the house which became the Fairoak Stores. The cottage has long since gone.

In the row beneath them are the teacher, Miss Lee, then John Humphreys, whose

Hilda"s parents Herbert and Ada Coppard ran Chessington's first newsagent's. See page 37.

Hilda Coppard lived at 2 Sunflower Cottages, Leatherhead Road, when this photograph was taken on her first day at school aged five.

home was the wartime "navvy" base at Ruxley Towers. Third from the left in the second row is Charlie Longhurst, who lived in a farm labourer's cottage on the green by Rushett Farm next to Rushett Dairy, Leatherhead Road. Next in the line is Bill Charman, who came from Almshouse Lane. Then there is Leslie Smithers, of Sunflower Cottages. Sixth from the left in the row is Frank Simmonds, also from Almshouse Lane. Seventh from the left is Arthur Peadle, whose home was opposite the cottages next to The Star, Malden Rushett, and adjacent to the "Iron Church". The lad on the far right, wearing a tie, is Reg Dolley, of Post Office Row, Leatherhead Road – opposite the entrance to the track which became Garrison Lane.

In the upper row of girls, on the far left is Violet Russell, also of Post Office Row. Next to her is Evelyn Moore, sister of the boys who lived in the wooden cottages next to the Fox and Hounds. Third from the left in the row is Olga Duffell, who lived at Hindhead – the end house in the row of cottages extending southwards from the Fox and Hounds, Leatherhead Road. Olga's mother was the village midwife. Fourth from the left is Violet Sayers, who resided at the brickfields, and whose mother, Elizabeth, ran the post office from 1926 to 1930. Fifth from the left is Bertha Wakeham, whose family lived over the road from The Harrow public house. Next to her is Emily Arnold, from Court Cottages, Leatherhead Road, close to where the Chessington Parade of shops was later built.

Seventh from the left is Mollie Holden. Her father was a keeper on Leatherhead golf course. She was a twin and the family lived in a "tiny" cottage on the course. Eighth from the left is Maude Harding, of Almshouse Lane.

In the bottom row are nine girls. The first, from left to right, is Alice Holder, twin sister of Mollie. The next is Thora Elmer. She was the daughter of a travelling shepherd, who only attended the school in the winter months when her family were required to mind the sheep at Leatherhead golf course. Then there is Evelyn Tomlinson, who dwelled in a cottage next door to Fair Oaks on the corner of Leatherhead Road and Rushett Lane.

Fourth from the left is Lorna Pead, whose home was one of the cottages on the green next to The Star. Next to her is Jessie Holloway, of Fair Oaks, before it was a shop. Sixth from the left in the bottom row is Ena Overington, from Almshouse Lane. Next to her is Betty Walters whose home was Montrose where the TVR motor showrooms traded in the 1990s.

Eighth from the left in the bottom row is Gladys Holloway, sister of Jessie, from Fair Oaks.

Finally, the girl on the far right in the bottom row is Mary Sayers, who lived at the Brickfields, opposite Whetstone's yard, Leatherhead Road.

Tragically, after leaving St Mary's School for a post at a larger school in Weybridge, headmaster Mr Brooker could not take the pressure. On a visit to relatives in Ashtead, he took his own life on the railway line one Christmas-time.

Pupils in class two at St Mary's Church of England School, Leatherhead Road, Chessington, on 11th January 1923. The teacher on the left is Miss Lee. On the far right is the headmaster, Mr Brooker. Most the pupils are named on the previous page.

The Stickleys

The Stickley family farmed many acres of Hook and North Chessington in the 19th and 20th centuries. John James Stickley examines a lark's nest at Buckland Road, long before the houses and school were built.

Men of Chessington prepare for trip in the 1920s by charabanc, parked outside The Harrow. The original public house was much smaller and was further back from the main road. There has been a pub on the site since at least the late 1700s.

Alongside the building was once a mortuary used by Kelsey's undertakers, opposite. If the mortuary was full, a little brick building was used in Almshouse Lane. One of those on this excursion is Nibby Saker, of Sunflower Cottages, who, with his wife, devoted his life to Chessington Cricket Club. A pavilion was named in his honour.

School and church next to public house
Star pupils

BEFORE 1865, when St Mary's C of E school was built in Leatherhead Road, children were educated at two other locations in Chessington.

One school was next door to the Star public house, Telegraph Hill, Malden Rushett. The other was nearer Hook, in Leatherhead Road, next to Court Cottages and was built in 1822 from money raised by subscription and could cater for up to 60 boys and girls. It also had a small schoolmaster's house attached. Here, classes were divided. One section was for those following the National School plan. The other was a middle school run by the Diocesan Board of Education for children of farmers and others. After it ceased being a school, it became H Peates' grocer's store and next door was Stag's Meadow once used for the village's cricket games. Mr Peates kept a horse that grazed in the meadow and wore leather shoes when working the cricket field.

At the "Star" school, the fee was 1d a week. Among the pupils in the late 1880s was William Thomas Bailey, who would arrive for lessons from the Rushett Dairy Farm just over the other side of Telegraph Hill in Leatherhead Road.

In her memoires, Mrs Hilda Pratt – formerly Hilda Coppard – recalls that at the age of 13, when her mother, father and seven brothers moved from Sunflower Cottages, Leatherhead Road, to a larger house, Woodview, next to The Star, she had a long walk to get to St Mary's School on the Leatherhead Road near Almshouse Lane.

"At the age of five *(in 1920)*, I was taken to St Mary's School from Sunflower Cottages and I remember passing the big house known as Burnt Stub. There was no such thing as Chessington Zoo or Chessington World of Adventures. My older brother was already a pupil at the school. There were nearly 100 on the register. The parish was said to cover several miles from end to end. Children from as far away as the Bones Gate came to the school where we stayed until we were 14.

"There were three classrooms, outside toilets, good cloakroom space, two playgrounds – one for boys and one for girls and infants. There was a house built into the school building where the headmaster, Mr Brooker, his wife and children lived.

"We were taken to school by horse and van. The carriage was one of Mr Whetstone's wood carts with planks along the side for seats and a tarpaulin over the top. There were very few cars in those days.

"The older boys came to school on their bikes. There were sheds for them at the back of the school. We were all taught

Proprietor, W. CROOK.   THE STAR INN, CHESSINGTON.   Good Accommodation for Travellers

The Star not only served as a public house in Victorian times. The adjoining "long room" on the right, was used as a school and church lectures were held there. The Reverend Chetwynd Staplyton sometimes had to walk 14 miles in wild weather to and from the parent church at Old Malden to conduct church lectures on the same day in Chessington and Malden Rushett. These were held here at The Star, and also at a cottage opposite the brickfield, Leatherhead Road, and at a cottage near the C of E school on the Leatherhead Road near Almshouse Lane.

reading, writing, arithmetic, religious instruction, needlework for girls and gardening for the boys. We celebrated May Day by dancing round the maypole suitably dressed for the occasion.

"By the time I had started to attend the school in 1920, Remembrance Day was celebrated. A war memorial was built into the school fence. The same memorial was later removed and installed at St Mary's Church. We laid a wreath on it each year for the victims of the war from the village. We had a flagpole in the playground and the head boy had to raise the flag on Empire Day while we all sang Rule Britannia, Britannia rules the waves. We also wore an oak leaf on Oak Apple Day.

"Standard III girls had cookery classes in the parish room built next door to the school playground. It had oil heating and lighting. We often had to take our food home, half-cooked, which did not please our mothers or make the class very interesting.

"We had mixed teaching for most of the lessons and lady teachers seemed to come from far away. I remember a Mrs Smithers, Miss Lee and Miss Sargent.

"The Francis Barker Recreation Ground next door to the school became well-used through the years. Lady Barker always came to the school to present prizes, and at the end of each school year she chose a boy school-leaver to work in her garden and a girl to work in the house."

Built for £1,000 but water from the well made children ill

A new school in Leatherhead Road

THE old National School in Leatherhead Road, near today's Chessington Parade shops, was in desperate need of repair by the late 1840s.

So, to raise the money for redecoration, the poorhouses at the end of Almshouse Lane were sold in 1849.

About this time, there were two schoolmasters – a Mr Kelsey and a Mr Bellchambers.

By 1865, Reverend Chetwynd Staplyton had acquired a site for a new school in Leatherhead Road, close to Almshouse Lane.

In modern times, four houses were built on the old school site next to the corrugated Chessington Parish Hall built in 1897 to commemorate the diamond jubilee of Queen Victoria.

Mr Staplyton arranged for the glebe land to be bought from Chessington's main landowner, Merton College, Oxford. New school buildings were constructed at a cost of £1,000 and were ready for the children to move into the following year. Teacher Mr Bellchambers was given £2 towards the cost of relocation.

The school committee decided to sell off the National School buildings further up the Leatherhead Road and these were purchased for £240 by Gordon Wyatt Clark, of Strawberry Hill, the large house in Leatherhead Road later known as Fleetwood and used by St Philip's School before demolition.

The new St Mary's School obtained an annual grant and HM inspectors visited the premises each year.

In August 1871, it was noted in the school log: "The examination (by the inspectors) has resulted on the whole fairly well, but the Arithmetic requires attention, especially at the Notation. Discipline is fairly efficient.

Needlework is good. Improvement must be made in Arithmetic throughout the school or the grant may have to be reduced next year."

By 1882, the school could afford to employ three teachers: Mr Bellchambers, Mr Kelsey's wife, Mary, and a new employee, Amelia Scott.

In 1885, Mr Bellchambers retired and his post was taken by a Mr Tozer. When Mr Bellchambers died a few years later, the whole parish felt the loss. His body was buried at St Mary's Church, Long Ditton.

Mr Tozer, who was headmaster in the late Victorian period.

Mr Bellchambers had held the post of schoolmaster and organist for 22 years and had been assistant overseer in Chessington, resigning in 1835.

Among the mourners at the funeral were Mr Chancellor, of Chessington Hall, and Stephen Humphrey of Guilders Hall Farm. The children from Chessington School lined the paths in the Long Ditton churchyard.

In 1894, after children became ill from water drawn from the school's well, a temporary supply was laid on from one of Mr Chancellor's cottages. Mr Tozer applied to the Lambeth Water Works Company at Long Ditton for water mains to be laid as far as the school and in the short-term, a cesspool and rainwater filter were deemed necessary.

Chessington School — Result of Christmas Examination 1909

Stand	Position	Name	Reading	Handwork Drawing	Compn	Dictn	Arith	Mental	Gramr	Geog	Writg	Gen K.	Spellg	Music	Total 240
VII	1	Walter Saker	19	20	20	20	20	18	19	18	16	15	19	18	222
	2	Henry Sayers	20	18	16	20	12	15	19	11	16	15	19	19	206
VI	1	Cissie Partridge	17	18	17	18	12	20	18	13	16	7	14	15	185
	2	Frank Styles	13	7	11	12	14	18	15	12	12	4	7	11	136
V	1	Hilda Cole	18	18	15	17	13	19	20	16	15	12	11	17	191
	2	Ruth Sayers	19	18	17	20	10	17	18	17	14	11	12	15	189
	3	Ebenr Sayers	15	14	16	18	14	18	17	18	11	13	11	17	182
	4	Alice Miles	17	19	15	19	6	14	17	15	19	8	11	10	170
	5	Rose Ansell	17	17	15	19	6	11	17	16	14	10	10	13	165
	6	Albert Hall	17	15	14	20	13	19	14	10	12	9	14	7	164
	7	Blanche Doughty	15	19	11	20	10	12	18	13	14	4	8	7	157
	8	Wm Westwood	16	14	15	10	13	18	19	12	12	3	8	11	151
	9	Olive Ayres	18	18	14	15	7	11	18	13	14	5	7	6	146
	10	Chas. Dolley	13	7	17	19	20	16	a	19	13	a	5	16	145
	11	Frances Overington	17	18	16	16	6	9	18	6	14	2	9	8	139
	12	Harry Mitchell	11	14	11	18	6	15	18	15	8	8	8	6	138
	13	Dorothy Ayres	16	16	17	16	4	12	17	12	10	5	6	5	136
	14	Daisy Dyer	11	19	15	16	11	15	14	13	13	8	a	a	135
IV	1	Annie Bailey	20	17	19	19	18	17	18	14	18	7	11	10	188
	2	Doris Meaden	19	18	17	19	14	20	16	10	14	6	9	5	167
	3	Eth. Partridge	18	20	11	14	14	12	16	7	13	4	6	9	144
	4	Winnie Coker	17	10	10	16	4	10	16	6	11	3	9	6	120
	5	Richd Holland	17	9	11	7	7	14	18	3	9	6	6	8	115
	6	Edwd Holland	10	11	10	13	7	10	16	5	10	2	5	7	107
	7	Fred Gocher	19	7	5	4	6	9	8	4	12	1	6	4	78
	8	Ernst Millard	7	12	6	7	0	8	9	0	4	2	1	2	64

A. T. Everard

How the pupils performed in 1909 at Chessington School.

St Mary's School in about 1937. Among the boys in the top row are Frank Styles, first on the left; "Boy" Fox, third from the left; Peter Sayers, fourth; Raymond Childs, fifth; Ernest Holder, sixth; "Boy" Clark, of Fairoak Lane, seventh; and last in the row, another Fox boy. In the bottom row are Joan Simmons, Joan Poulton, Graham Green, Betty Bishop, Freda Gocher, Jean Farmer, Cynthia Toms, Margaret Bailey, Audrey Truscott, of Acre Hill Farm, and a girl as yet unidentified. The small boy in the middle is Kenny White. He "never grew any taller and despite appearing rather ill and thin was the brainiest in the school".

The Blacka-moor's Head, Moor Lane, after the rail-way's arrival.

First trains to Chessington

A train in public service arrives at Chessington South Station, Garrison Lane, on 28th May 1939, the first day of operation.

SOUTHERN Region had obtained an Act of Parliament in 1930 to build a railway from Motspur Park to Leatherhead, by way of Tolworth and Chessington.

The area was rapidly becoming residential and rail links to London were deemed essential. Work started in 1936 and provided much entertainment for Hook and Chessington's children as bridges were built in Bridge Road, Cox Lane and Moor Lane. Youngsters delighted in watching trucks carrying construction materials trundling down the lines. Trespassing by children was a problem. The first section to Tolworth opened on 15th May 1938 and the length to Chessington followed on 14th May 1939 with trains put into public use a fortnight later.

Originally it was planned to call Chessington North Station "Chessington Court", after the nearby farm which stood on what is now the Holmwood Road estate in Hook. The name for Chessington South was to be called "Chessington Grange" after the house at the corner of Garrison Lane and Leatherhead Road occupied by Alderman Bridge.

The railway line was due to continue to Leatherhead and work began south of Garrison Lane to beyond Chalky Lane. The war intervened and new Green Belt restrictions some years later which restricted residential development in the countryside, thwarted Southern Region's plans.

In the early 1930s it was intended to build a new town like Harlow at Malden Rushett. It thankfully did not materialise and the railway remains a branch line linking Chessington with Tolworth, Wimbledon, Clapham Junction and Waterloo. An extension to Leatherhead has periodically been called for.

Old Mr Whetstone, who kept a woodyard in Leatherhead Road, conveyed the village children to Chessington School in his horse-drawn carriage during the 1920s. He kept a whip in case there were any discipline problems arising among the youngsters. His furthest collection point was outside the Star, Malden Rushett. Mr Whetstone could not read or write until the day he died.

Key dates in zoo history

DURING 1930, entrepreneur Reginald S Goddard, a flight lieutenant in the Great War, decided to embark on a new venture in his life. He was the managing director of his family's Battersea-based slate and slab firm, specialising in producing slate billiard tables, but also worked for some years in insurance after leaving school at Ongar, Essex.

R S Goddard opened up a chain of billiard halls around London and one was apparently leased to a pet shop which stocked out-of-the-ordinary species that attracted much public interest.

The knowledge that there could be a good living to be made by exhibiting animals stemmed from this business deal with the pet store.

Mr Goddard, or "RS" as he was known, thought about starting up a zoo, and on a drive from Kingston to Leatherhead, spotted land for sale at Chessington. The zoo's history is summarised in this brief chronology, partly made possible by the extensive research carried out over a lifetime by C H Keeling in his publication, The Chessington Story.

•**1931**: Surrey Zoological Gardens opened in July.

•**1932**: Concern by Epsom Rural District councillors over number of advertising hoardings along Leatherhead Road and unauthorised motorised tea canteens at the roadside.

•**1933**: Maps still refer to zoo as Surrey Zoological Gardens.

•**1935**: Disastrous fire in stables at 4am on 29th

Chessington Zoo seen from the air in the 1950s. The car park is top left and the circus, right.

September. Five ponies, including Nancy and Squibbs, and a zebra, Charlie, perish in flames. A plaque later commemorated them.

•**1936**: Advert tells of animals and their names – Joey the monkey in a circus on a tightrope, Teddy bear, lions, cubs, elephant, tigers, leopards, hyenas and bears tea party, as well as penguins, ostriches, flamingoes, a zebra and two sealions. Some 200,000 visitors during the season.

•**1937**: New arrivals include tigers, spotted hyenas, another pair of camels. Improved entrance, larger car park.

•**1938**: Babies expected in zebra and sealion departments. Tiger cubs named Snip, Snap and Snorum. Wallabies and kangaroos have young in their pouches. Penguins breeding.

•**1939**: Government restrictions at start of war lead to temporary closure of zoo, as part of a programme of preventing large crowds forming at entertainment venues during wartime.

•**1941**: Chessington amalgamated with Paignton Zoo to become Chessington and Devon Zoo during war period. An elephant, lions and tigers went to Devon. Frank Foster, famous circus ringmaster taken on at Chessington as circus manager and equestrian director. Circus had 36 horses and ponies, three elephants, two camels, a pair of llamas, a mule, three monkeys, a sealion and "12 pretty West End chorus girls".

•**1944**: During the war years, 21 bombs fell in the grounds, and three people were killed. A doodlebug exploded in a tree above the polar bear cage, ripping off a door; a monkey cage was blown apart, allowing the terrified animals to flee the scene before recapture some days later; penguin enclosure destroyed and an ostrich's leg was severed and flung 30 feet, necessitating the termination of the creature's life. Jack, the polar bear, was thrust against the side of his cage by the blast and lay silent, bedazzled and blackened for days, but miraculously recovered.

•**1945**: Contract with Devon finishes as war ends. Animals and staff return to Chessington from Paignton.

- **1946**: R S Goddard dies on Christmas Day. Chessington Zoological Garden becomes a company. The 1,500 animals consume daily 30 tons of meat, 60 boxes of bananas, 40 boxes of oranges, and require 20 tons of straw for bedding.
- **1947**: Harry Snazle, newly discharged from the army, takes over catering. By now visitors each year consume 9,000 gallons of ice cream.
- **1953**: The roaring of lions could be heard at night as far away as Clayton Road, Hook. Increasing traffic later muffled their cries.
- **1957**: Zoo succeeds in breeding the blue and yellow macaw. Harry Snazle is by now director of the zoo.
- **1962-3**: Polar bears at home in the Arctic winter conditions of of 1962-3. Giraffes join zoo collection. A Chessington hybrid caused a sensation when a Watussi bull and an American bison cow bred, producing two cows. It was believed to have been a world first. By now, a large grassy area fronting the Leatherhead Road contained the lions and tigers. A zebra, born in the notoriously foggy December of 1962, was named Smog. By now a new attraction was a common hippopotamus, Humphrey.
- **1965**: Happy, the giraffe, allegedly named after one of Snow White's seven dwarfs, died in November.
- **1967-70**: Ape house opened. Deputy director Eddie Orbell quits after many years to run a wildlife park in Scotland. The zoo now has 335 mammals in 101 species; 800 birds in 103 species; 51 reptiles and amphibians and 200 fish in 21 and 70 species respectively.
- **1972**: Death of Hans Brick at the age of 72 on 22nd August in Middlesex. He had built the circus at Chessington. Stock is 406 mammals in 103 species; 568 birds in 136 species; 28 reptiles and amphibians in 19 and 58 species respectively. Bird garden work in progress. Collection included jackals, leopards, pumas, wolves, coyotes, racoons, mongooses, cranes, flamingoes and storks.
- **1973**: Gift shop staff told: "Don't help children put films in camera unless they have bought the rolls at the store". Claud, a wiry pensioner working in the shop, excels at dealing with abusive youths banging the penny amusement machines behind the shop.
- **1975**: Harry Snazle still in charge, but dies in the late 1970s.
- **1978**: Pearson's, a subsidiary of the Tussaud Group, buys zoo. First manager is Peter Morgan.
- **1980**: Head keeper is Ron "Ginger" Eaton, replaced later by Chris Anscombe, previously head primate

Pets corner at Chessington Zoo in the 1940s. Inset: Zoo founder Reginald Goddard.

keeper. Nigel Martin, an ex-Royal Marines officer takes over as manager, assisted by Robin Dunham and David Attwood, who both leave the zoo's employment by 1991.
- **1981**: Former elephant keeper Lionel Rowe becomes zoo manager.
- **1987**: Plans launched by Pearson's to turn the zoo into a theme park and rename it Chessington World of Adventures.
- **1990**: Baby gorilla born at Chessington in January. Shani was born to Kumba II and Lomie.
- **1996**: Dennis Vrettos and David Herbert, who started working at the zoo in 1988, were among the keepers still in employment.
- **1998**: Lionel Rowe due to retire.
- **1999**: Exciting new adventure ride opened.

Gone are the zoo's elephants, giraffes, hippopotamus, orang-utans, llamas, bison, deer, pelicans and the large vulture-type bald eagle so often seen from the Leatherhead Road.

The tea room at Burnt Stub in the 1940s.

Cans of milk on the bicycle handlebars

Rushett Dairy Farm

IN THE 1870s, a young man from Tolworth could be seen pedalling through Hook and Chessington on a tricycle on his way to work. He was Edward Bailey.

Edward's first job was as a painter on the Lord Foley estate at Claygate and his skills at the profession brought promotion to foreman.

Later, however, he took over the Rushett Dairy where he moved in about 1880 on marrying Sarah Anne Ambrose, a cook and housekeeper at a large house next to The Fishponds in Ewell Road, Surbiton. Sarah had come from the Sudbury area of Suffolk.

At first, Edward and Sarah kept only "two or three cows", according to their granddaughter, Betty. But soon, their little dairy "grew and grew" until in later years, they managed a commercial herd of 50 cattle, expanding to an accredited herd of 80 Scottish Ayres. They were transported from Scotland by road at night to Byhurst Farm, which the ambitious Bailey family had taken over just before the start of the Second World War as part of their plans for the dairy's growth.

By then, the Baileys were renting some of their 500 acres of land off Merton College and also from Southern Railway, since some of the countryside around Chalky Lane had already been bought by the railway company when it was intended to expand the line south to Leatherhead from Chessington South station. The railway was not extended because the war intervened and the plans were put on hold, never to be realised. A small bridge had been constructed over Chalky Lane for the trucks to transport materials. The line went right through the Baileys' farm.

By now, most of Malden Rushett and further afield was being supplied with the Baileys' milk, delivered by hand in cans. Pints and half pints were poured into jugs at customers' homes. Before the start of the war, the herd was laboriously milked by hand.

Edward and Sarah Bailey had five children. The sons were Edward James, born 1881; Walter Frederick, born 1882; and William Thomas, born in 1884. There were two daughters – Daisy and Annie. Some of the family helped on the dairy farm, particularly brothers Walter and William. Edward, however, went away to work.

Walter married and had two children, William and Margaret. From William Thomas's marriage were four children, Betty, Mary, Joan and Charles. In retirement, Betty (Rhodes) lived at 260

Farmers Walter Bailey and his brother, William, at Rushett Dairy Farm in August 1929.

Hook Road, Hook.

Betty recalled that on Guy Fawkes' night, a bonfire was lit on the small common outside Rushett Farm Cottages, near the dairy, and most of the village used to turn up for the celebrations.

"All the lads who went to the school near Almshouse Lane came along. It was good," she said.

"Our cows used to graze on the common by the farm but we also had to take them up the Leatherhead Road to the four fields where the Chessington Nurseries set up.

"My father and uncle used to get up at 3.30 in the morning to cut the hay and then do the milking by hand.

"When the war came we had to have the fields ploughed up by tractor. It was a marvellous way of life those days", said Betty, whose family lived in Byhurst Farm cottages off Fairoak Lane.

There was major interruption to the farm in the war. Twenty-two high explosive bombs fell in the farm's fields as well as three landmines and numerous incendiary devices.

In the 1930s, the Leatherhead Road had a good number of refreshment stops for the many cyclists and hikers. One was Mrs Ida Copp's refreshment rooms at Hillcroft, the most northern of the little row of cottages and houses next to The Star pub,

Telegraph Hill. Mrs Copp had a tea garden at the back with umbrellas for customers to sit under. She would often need extra milk for her thirsty visitors. This was brought to her by Betty Bailey's mother, on a bicycle, the cans being positioned on each handlebar.

Another tea house opened in Star Cottages, next door to The Star, recalled Betty. The Long Room adjoining the Star also served tea and squash to the many people stopping on coach trips to and from the coast.

Mrs Copp was a matron at one of the local hospitals in addition to her work with the tourists' Sunday afternoon teas.

Betty said there was possibly yet another cottage in the row which served teas and minerals for a time. Teas were also served at the Fair Oaks shop on the corner of Leatherhead Road and Rushett Lane when it was run by Mr and Mrs Harold Pywell. Mr Pywell served as a councillor with the local authority. The garden at the back was laid out with tables for the cyclists to use on their way to either Epsom Downs or Oxshott Woods. Refreshments were available also at the cafe next to Kelsey's forge; in Leatherhead Road between the Harrow and Mansfield Road; at Chalky Lane; Walton Cottage; and also at Post Office Row in Rose Childs' shop which later became Barwell Cafe.

Cows from Rushett Dairy Farm grazed on the common beside Leatherhead Road.

Edward and Sarah Bailey. They started Rushett Dairy Farm soon after moving into the cottage off Leatherhead Road in 1880.

Some of the cattle and a hayrick at Rushett Dairy Farm, Malden Rushett, between the wars.

Puzzle of a name kept alive on the buses

Copt Gilders Farm

WHEN people see the name Copt Gilders on the bus timetable or on the route 71 double-deckers as they weave around the Gilders Road estate they must sometimes wonder about the origins of the name.

Copt Gilders referred to the centuries-old farmhouse which stood in what is now Hemsby Road. It used to stand where the first bend is in the road when approaching from Church Lane. Some householders say they are still turning up old bricks from the building when digging in their gardens.

In his unpublished work on the history of Chessington, carried out in the 1970s, D J Field cast some light on the history of the name. The old farm was pulled down in the 1930s and its land of some 250 acres was sold to developers for a large housing estate. The author wrote that the farm used to be the manor house for land at Chessington owned by Merton Abbey, and would have been lived in by the estate manager monks. The manor used to be known as Fryerne or Frierne. "Later, the house inexplicably became known as Copp Guilders. Copp refers to the summit of a hill and the guilders to yellow flowers that grew there." In 1288 Father Peter was in charge of the manor.

Researcher Bryan Randell wrote in 1976 that in 1839, it was known as Cap Gilders Hall. He said a cap is old English for cup, and its occupant may have gilded church chalices or "copps" and was a "copt gilder".

There were two manor houses close to each other – Copt Guilders (Friern) and Chessington, whose manor house was Chessington Hall. Another manor was the lesser-known "Chessington at Hoke (Hook)".

In the 1660s, what became known as Copt Gilders farm, was possibly the largest building in the parish of Chessington, since taxes were thought to have been paid on eight hearths in the property. This was more than twice that of any other building in the parish.

A view of Copt Gilders Farm which was pulled down in the 1930s.

A 71 bus to Copt Gilders in 1998.

A different view of the farm buildings.

Copt Gilders farmhouse in its final few years.

William Pywell was running Chessington post office from this house, Fair Oaks, in the 1930s. He also opened tea gardens at the rear.

Did you know that . . .?

UNTIL a few years ago, The Star public house, Malden Rushett, was four-fifths in the London borough of Kingston, and one fifth in Mole Valley. The rates had to be divided. The pub had an Oxshott phone number and the postal address was Kingston Road, Leatherhead. The postmen arrived from Leatherhead, but the property and the cottages around it, are in the parish of Chessington. Before 1884, they were in Malden parish.

In the late 1920s, the nearest newsagent's was at Seymour's at Southborough, Hook. Chessington was an outlandish place

to get papers to, so Herbert Coppard decided to become a newsagent. Newspapers were dropped off on the doorstep of Myrtle Cottages, but the landlady, Mrs Annie Whetstone, would not allow them to be sold from the house. When the Coppards moved to Wood View, Telegraph Hill, the newspapers were sold from his family's house. Herbert delivered most the newspapers on the way to work at the Epsom mental hospitals. His wife, Ada, and family helped him. Sweets, cigarettes and tobacco were also sold from Wood View house.

Most of Malden Rushett has always had Epsom phone numbers. In the case of fire, an engine is usually sent from Epsom.

Rushett Filling Station in 1958.

When Chessington South station opened in 1939, an old-style horse-bus ferried customers to and from Chessington Zoo. Later, the 65A bus did the horses' work and this novelty transport was discontinued. Once, in the 1960s, police attended an accident outside the zoo caused by a stray penguin colliding with a taxi. PC Michael Burgess took the bird into custody and "released" it in the foyer of Surbiton police station causing the duty sergeant much distress..

Granny Smith's sweet shop, Post Office Row, Leatherhead Road. After 1930, Rose Childs ran a grocer's shop at the premises and later, she served teas on wooden tables. This cottage, where Chessington post office traded from about 1890 to 1914, became Barwell Cafe in later years and has been partly modernised. Rose's daughter, Barbara, still lived at the premises in 1999. The other cottages were demolished. Barbara once recalled how her mother used to feed buns to Rosie the elephant being exercised along the road outside. One day when Mrs Childs was too busy to hand a bun to Rosie, the animal scooped up some muddy water in her trunk and hosed it down the front of the shop "in protest".

Post Office Row, pictured in 1889, was in Leatherhead Road opposite the junction of the track which became Garrison Lane.

Post Office Row and Granny Smith's sweet shop

THIS fine old photograph of Post Office Row is from a set taken by John Tims in 1889. He pedalled around the neighbourhood on a penny farthing bicycle taking pictures of everyday life within a few miles of his home in Chessington Road. In the 1920s, schoolgirl Hilda Coppard used to go behind the counter in Granny's Smith's sweet shop and make small "twists" out of newspaper to hold the confectionery purchased. "There were jars and jars of lovely sweets including coconut squares," she recalled many years later.

"Granny Smith was a tiny thing. We would run up there in the dinner hour at school and spend a halfpenny or a penny on sweets and then play in the tree plantation next door, which we called The Planny."

In the 1930s, Colonel Derek Richardson ran Chessington Grange riding school from Garrison Lane.

In 1954, the gravel lane was suddenly tarmacadamed "within four days". The next day the Queen arrived at Chessington South station on her way to the Derby.

Deer chased for miles

Hunting days

STAG hunting was a popular pastime for the area's gentry. For many years up to 1905, the West Surrey Hunt was based at Rushett Farm.

The building of extra houses and cottages in the late Victorian and Edwardian period hampered the hunt's activities and it was finally decided to auction off the animals and the kennels.

"Large and ever-widening areas over which the hounds were to be seen in full cry only a few years ago have been radically changed through the influence of the speculative builder," reported the Surrey Comet at the time.

The hunt was reported to have been started by "Squire" Blake, who lived at Malden, when his harriers once got on the track of a deer. However, a Mr W Hoare is also referred to in other documents. In the 1880s, the sport reached its zenith of popularity. There were "some grand old days" with the master, Sir David Evans, of Ewell, a former Lord Mayor of London, and Billy Poole as hard-riding huntsman.

Sir David's successors in the mastership were Mr W Twigg (1892-1895); Mr E H d'Avigdor (1895-6) – killed in the hunting field; Mr Martin D Rucker (1896-1899); Mr A J Curnick (1899-1903); and Mr Ernest Robinson, of Claygate, (1903-1905). Under Mr Robinson, the best run on record – six hours – was attained.

Once, a deer was chased as far away as Thames Ditton and

The hunt outside The Harrow, Leatherhead Road, in the early 1930s. The pub was kept by Henry and Eliza Pridmore. Inset: The kennels at Rushett Farm, Chessington, in 1901 before the West Surrey Hunt closed down in 1905.

Hampton Court.

The winding up of the West Surrey Hunt at Rushett Farm did not spell the end of hunting in Chessington. For several years until well into the 1930s, the sport was carried on from kennels next to the Harrow public house.

The kennel keeper, Mr Benham, was said to have taken his own life when the hunt was eventually forced to disband.

Fox hunt beagles set off from the kennels next to the Harrow public house, Leatherhead Road, Chessington, in about 1930.

Stuart Whetstone at the age of 14 in 1907.

Fairoak Cottages, home to the Whetstones for decades.

Stuart and Kit Whetstone at the woodyard on their golden wedding anniversary in 1973. They were married at St Mary's, Chessington, in 1923.

Ann Whetstone, right, with a friend at her family's woodyard.

Fairoak Cottages in 1985 before being boarded up.

Pear Tree Bungalow, Leatherhead Road, where a family of five slept in one room in the early 1930s. The pebbledashed cottage was demolished in the 1980s.

Working hard at Whetstone's woodyard

THE name Whetstone has been linked with Chessington since the 19th century. For the majority of this time, the Whetstone family's focal point was the woodyard in Leatherhead Road, where they traded up until the early 1980s when the business was sold.

Reverend Chetwynd Staplyton, in his Victorian diaries, wrote of one particular ancestor of the family.

"Mrs Whetstone was another peculiar old woman who lived at the Rushett. Her son had slept in her room from his childhood and no one else was known to have entered within her door. She even drove the rent collector from her house.

"At the age of 40, her son, James, alias Jemmy, fell in love with a tidy young woman and offered marriage.

"Mrs Taylor, the young woman's mother, insisted upon cleaning the house, and after one day with a hoe, and two days scrubbing, she consented to her daughter's marriage. But the old lady *(Mrs Whetstone)* was broken-hearted and died a few days after the marriage."

Born in 1864 was another colourful character, "Whiff Whaff" Whetstone, who could not read or write throughout his life. His wife, Ann, was born in 1866 and died aged 74 in 1935 – just four days after her husband.

"Whiff Whaff" Whetstone used to take the children of Rushett to Chessington School in a horse-drawn carriage covered with a tarpaulin. The youngsters delighted in this mode of transport along the quiet Leatherhead Road when there were barely any motor vehicles on the highway. "Whiff Whaff" carried a whip should any of the young boys start to cause trouble. This old Chessington character is fondly remembered for his tendency to dribble down his waistcoat and his hatred of motor cars.

Ann and Stuart, son of "Whiff Waff", took over the school run in the 1920s, and conveyed children to school from as far away as the Star, Malden Rushett. "Whiff Whaff" and his wife were buried at Chessington Church on 21st February 1935.

Stuart Whetstone, born in 1892, left school in 1906, when Queen Victoria's son, King Edward VII, was on the throne. In this year, some new cottages were being built in the Leatherhead Road almost opposite the woodyard. They included Heath Cottage. Built a few years earlier was Myrtle Cottages, a few doors north of Heath Cottage. In November 1904, these cottages were put up for sale by Messrs White and Son at Leatherhead, but they went unsold at the time.

Stuart Whetstone married Eliza Matilda – or "Kit" as she was known – at St Mary's Church, Chessington, on April 28, 1923. They had met at Chessington. Stuart joined the West Kent Regiment at the beginning of the 1914-18 war and while serving, was wounded three times.

With the 18th Middlesex Regiment, he was awarded the Military Medal.

Stuart and Kit had three children, Donald, born 1926, Ann, born 1927, and William, born 1929.

Initially, the family lived at Pear Tree Bungalow at the woodyard, which was demolished 50 years later, and from 1934, they resided at Fairoak Cottages, boarded up in the 1990s.

Ann Whetstone, who became Ann Sayers, upon marrying, recalled in retirement her childhood days at Pear Tree Bungalow and Fairoak Cottages.

"Pear Tree Bungalow was like a little wooden-floored scout hut or a First World War hut," she said. "There was only one bedroom which all the family shared. As you walked into the bungalow, you were in the kitchen with a sink in the right-hand corner. A step led to the living room. The wall separating the bedroom did not reach the ceiling and you could hear what was going on.

"Outside was a ditch which was partly culverted. We had to walk across a plank to get to the front door of the bungalow. We'd put our wellies on and go up the tunnel. If you were brave enough – and one boy was – you could come out at Rushett Lane by Epsom Lane *(now Rushett Lane).*

"I got half way and turned back. The pipe came down from the fields and it was open at first as it went past the Sakers' home at Sunflower Cottages. Then it was brought across the road to our side.

"There was no electricity. We used lamps and fires".

Ann Whetstone, born in 1860, at the family woodyard in Leatherhead Road, Chessington.

The Whetstones had an outdoor toilet in the back yard. A guard dog "with starry eyes which glowed in the dark was tied up by the closet".

Upon the death of "Whiff Whaff" they moved across the woodyard to Fairoak Cottages. By now, hard work was the order of the day for the youngsters. Ann said: "If you had the wireless on, my father would turn it off and said: 'Work first, pleasure after!' He even threw a library book I was reading into the fire."

Five in a bed

WHEN Stuart Whetstone returned from the First World War, he found his father's woodyard business in a run-down state. Because his father was illiterate, the paperwork had mainly gone by the board.

Stuart took over the business and also ran the horse-drawn school bus for a few years until the service was taken over by Luff's of Leatherhead. Luff's operated from a site which became Hardy's Engineering close to where B&Q, the DIY superstore, was built in modern times. Luff's ran the service commercially and when Moor Lane School opened in 1936, Luff's expanded their service.

When Stuart's father, "Whiff Whaff" died, the coffin was taken to St Mary's Church in a horse-drawn hearse.

During the war, Stuart and Kit Whetstone, along with other villagers, took in children from the bomb-prone London districts. Two youngsters called, Grace and Tich, from Shoreditch, in the the East End, stayed with the Whetstones at 4 Fairoak Cottages.

The girls, together with the Whetstone's own two sons and a daughter, slept in the same bed – the three girls at the top of the bed and the two boys at the bottom. The Whetstone children's father even had to share a bed with his eldest sister for a time. So many people were in the house that it got confusing. When Stuart Whetstone went to punish his daughter, Ann, for accidentally setting fire to some hay on the farm, he struck the wrong child because they had swapped places in bed. There was no

William, Donald, Bill and Stuart Whetstone in the flourishing days of the woodyard.

electricity in Fairoak Cottages, just paraffin lamps.

The woodyard was sold to Champion's in about 1982, after Trevor, Stuart's grandson, chose not to continue the family firm.

Dangers of the saw mill and Bob Monkhouse's visit

WORKING at a saw mill is a hazardous occupation as Chessington's Whetstone family knew.

Stuart Whetstone lost the top of his finger in one accident. In another, Donald, his son, carved his hand on the saw. And Stuart's other son, William, was involved in a frightening incident when carving a name on a piece of thin wood owned by a customer. Suddenly the saw slipped and "there was blood everywhere".

William's mother, Kit, wrapped her son's hand in a towel and he was rushed to Epsom District Hospital and had numerous stitches. Surgeons at first thought the might have to amputate his hand.

The woman customer drove off after the accident with-

out offering assistance but her husband rang up the same evening inquiring as to William's welfare.

Soon after the saws changed from being petrol-driven to working on electricity, the young comedian Bob Monkhouse arranged to come down to the woodyard to make a "Mad Movie" film.

He wore a white suit and the film producers strapped him on a long platform and pushed him towards the revolving circular saw. One of the young woodyard workers stood by the switch and was instructed when to turn it off. Stuart Whetstone was most concerned at the stunt. So, too, was Bob Monkhouse. He apparently drank a half bottle of whisky first.

Stuart and Kit Whetstone with grandsons Trevor Whetstone and Barry Sayers in about 1959.

Chessington residents celebrate the end of the Second World War in 1945 with a VE day party in Fairoak Lane.

Childhood memories

BETTY Smith was born in her parents' bed in their cottage, Haslemere, on Leatherhead Road, Malden Rushett, in 1917. Submarine warfare was at its height in the First World War, food was short and Lord Kitchener had recently drowned.

She was the third daughter of Frederick and Mary Smith. A son, Sydney George, followed 18 months later.

Mr Smith was a golf course architect working for Carters' Seeds. He and his wife were forced to return from his work at Dieppe when the war broke out.

In retirement at Corscombe, Dorset, Betty Smith (married name Odell), wrote fondly and vividly – of her childhood at Chessington.

"We had neither electricity nor gas; just one cold water tap in the house, above a shallow stone sink in the scullery. There was no lavatory indoors, just a bucket under a substantial wooden seat in an outhouse reached by the back door. There was disinfectant in the bucket so it did not smell too bad. It was one of the jobs of us children to cut newspapers into squares, make a hole in the corner, thread through a piece of string and hang them in the lavatory for family use.

"My poor father had to dig a hole at the bottom of the garden – an area forbidden to us – to bury the bucket's contents. I never heard him complain.

"In the kitchen was a big range with coal fire, oven and hob. A big black kettle seemed always to be ready to provide hot water for washing or making cups of tea for the grown-ups. Round the range stood a sturdy and protective brass-edged fire guard upon which perpetually hung garments, and in the early years, no doubt, nappies airing. Here, mother did all the cooking. There was also the big dresser and scrubbed table and chairs. This was where all the family meals were taken.

"Under the top of this table was a narrow shelf where we children put the bits of food that we did not like. I hated fat.

"I remember when the war ended, seeing a stranger at the table and noticing this strange pair of black boots he was wearing. I was frightened. It was not daddy. I howled. It turned out to be Uncle William who had returned from serving his country in India.

"Each morning we looked out for Bill Bailey, the milkman. His horse and cart would stop outside the house. The cart was very dirty, having come from a wet, dung-covered farmyard. Old Bill

This cottage which stood in Rushett Lane, opposite the Fair Oaks up until the 1930s, was the home of the Day family in the 1920s. It was demolished and there is just a paddock in its place. The view is looking north towards Chessington and Hook. Inset: Betty Smith in 1921.

limped heavily, wore a funny old hat and looked quite unwashed. He stomped up to the back door carrying his pail of milk, previously ladled out of the big churn on the milkcart. Mother would be at the door with two clean jugs and into these, old Bill ladled and measured with metal containers, hung on the side of the pail, the ordered fresh pints of milk from the hand-milked cows.

"All cows were known by name. There was Daisy, Buttercup and Bluebell, to name just three. We learnt how to milk the cows ourselves. It was a happy and carefree time of our life.

"Very rarely did a doctor call at the house. Medicines were few and simple. For cuts, iodine was applied, and we squealed because it stung. We usually had bare legs, so often we grazed our knees. Frequently, wounds went septic and a linseed poultice would be applied every four hours or so. Linseed was heated in a saucepan with a little water. Bandages were torn off old sheets.

"For lighting in the house we had candles and matches. Oh! the fun of taking candles to bed and seeing how they flickered and made exciting changing patterns! Downstairs were two Aladdin lamps with fragile mantles fuelled by paraffin. The only heat in the house was from the kitchen range and a coal fire in

Oxshott (Fairoak) Lane in Edwardian times.

the living room.

"Mother would walk us to Oxshott Woods and on the way back would complain about our weight. Then she would find our pockets full of sand from the Oxshott woods sandpits.

"During the General Strike the bus to Leatherhead would stop outside the house to take me to school. I remember the bus's windows were broken. They had been smashed by strikers protesting at students driving them.

"Mrs Duffell lived next door. 'Duff' was the midwife and was a wonderful help."

Monk Cottage

MONK Cottage (above) formerly known as Rose Cottage is one of Chessington's oldest surviving buildings. It dates back to the late 1500s and is three-quarters of a mile south of Chessington Church. Even in modern times is surrounded by farmland and belies the fact it is situated in a Greater London borough.

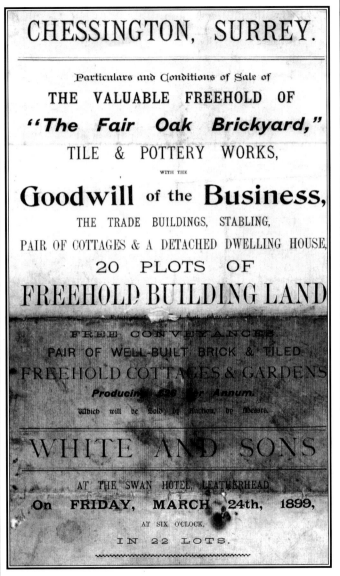

The lane it faces was the road from Chessington to Ashtead and Leatherhead, but this is now just a path and bridleway known as Green Lane.

The cottage, which in 1999 was beautifully kept with picture-postcard gardens and miniature waterfalls, was one of the few remaining timber-framed buildings in the area.

The earliest part of the cottage appears to be the central smoke bay building of three bays, according to a survey carried out in 1977 by the Surrey Domestic Buildings Research Group.

There is a blocked doorway into the western room but the original door may well have been elsewhere. Access to the to the smoke bay is through a cupboard to the south of the present chimney and then down between this and the west face of the smoke bay to a void on the north side.

Here, the soot-encrusted timbers with their daub infill remained until modern times.

The outlet for the smoke was in the east gable, evidenced by the blackening of the rafters.

Many of the exposed external timbers have been replaced and the ground floor has been underbuilt in brick.

In about 1900, a large wing was added to the north east corner of Monk Cottage and built in Gothic style. Inside, reused carved timbers, said to have come from Winchester Cathedral, were used. At this time, the front door was moved. Historians noted in 1977 that the vestry door in Chessington Church was said to have also come from Winchester Cathedral.

In the 1950s, further alterations were carried out at the cottage to link two different parts of the house.

Flower pot makers

An auction was held in Leatherhead on 24th March 1899 to find a buyer for the freehold and business of the Fair Oak Brickyard, Tile and Pottery works at Leatherhead Road, Chessington.

Michael Emery worked as a potter in the early days of the Fair Oaks tile works.

A POTTERY business, for much of the time producing flower pots, operated from premises in the Leatherhead Road. It was 300 yards south of the Fairoak crossroads, a short distance from the present day West Road junction. In the 1930s, Ebenezer Sayers, a Zionist, ran the business. "Ebie" Sayers' first wife died and he remarried. He had a son, George, who lived in West Road, and another in Leatherhead Road. One of his two daughters suffered from a club foot. In the 1930s, numerous members members of the Sayers family lived in Malden Rushett, occupying South View Cottages, Minnick Wood, Rose Cottage, Cranley and Shanklin. The works eventually closed. It is said the claypit at the back of the works Epsom salts, traces of which helped the plants put in the flower pots. When rivals firms learnt of this, they added Epsom salts to their own clay.

Bridge Road was laid out in 1937 and named after Councillor Clement H Bridge, a prominent member of Surbiton Urban District Council who lived at Chessington Grange, a house in Leatherhead Road with an orchard and meadow. It is now the site of Burton Close.

Frederick and Ivy Chatfield's general store near the Bonesgate in the late 1930s. The building has long since been pulled down and Chessington Hill Park estate has been built in its place.

Moor Lane looking towards Chatfield's provisions shop near the Bonesgate, in about 1938. Children drank water from a well behind the shop on their way home from school on hot summer afternoons.

One of the old cottages near the Bonesgate which has now vanished.

Hard to believe it's in a London borough
Rushett Farm

RUSHETT Farm's history dates back to as early as 1264 and is referred to in the accounts of Merton Priory's affairs. The five-bedroom farmhouse of later times is set back from the Leatherhead Road and dates back to the early part of the 1600s. Its design was quite common for the period.

From this charming period building, still owned by Merton College, along with Park Farm, there are views over some 700 acres of farmland. It is difficult to imagine that officially it is in the London borough of Kingston upon Thames. Only the distant landmark of Tolworth Tower interrupts this rural landscape.

Hundreds of years ago, land at Rushett Farm was "grubbed out" by pigs and man. Timber from its woods was used in London to build ships.

Between the wars, the farm was kept by Harold Prewett, a farmer who did not write down anything but "kept it in his brains".

In 1927, the adjoining Park Farm was taken over by former First World War naval officer Jack Woodall and his wife, Phyllis.

Jack hailed from Burslem, one of the towns in the Staffordshire Potteries region. His wife came from a small village near Bishops Stortford, Herts. They met due to the fact that Phyllis's sister had married Jack's brother.

After the Great War, Jack left the navy and trained at an agricultural college. When qualified, he took on Park Farm, where his son, Bart, was born in 1929.

At the beginning of the Second World War, the Woodalls left Chessington and bought Highlands Farm between Headley and Leatherhead.

"They needed to expand, and at that time the rents were low," Bart recalled many years later.

In 1948, the Woodalls took over Rushett Farm from the Prewetts. The Woodalls had three children, Richard, Guy and Sally. Richard kept Park Farm in the 1990s and Guy ran Thorncroft Vineyard, Leatherhead.

Phyllis Woodall was a keen supporter of Chessington Church and the family were to become mainstays of the Rushett area for the rest of the century.

At the age of 70, Bart was still running Rushett Farm as the millennium approached. For more than 15 years, he owned a light aircraft and regularly made trips to Europe.

Even more remotely situated in Chessington is Acre Hill Farm, off Chalky Lane, whose cottages are said to have been originally constructed in the 12th century.

Rushett Farm in the summer of 1999. The farmhouse dates back to the early 1600s.

Malden Rushett used to have a Sunday School mission hall behind the cottages next to Rushett Filling Station. Services were led in the 1940s by evangelists Philip and Eleanor Elliott, of Claygate. The building – gas lamps in place – still stood in 1999 in Evelyn and Ron Rapley's garden (left).

Bart Woodall in 1976.

Phyllis Woodall with a shire horse carrying her son, Guy, in about 1959. The horse was used to convey milk from Acre Hill Farm to Park Farm.

Chessington bombed

FIFTY-SIX people died in the borough of Surbiton during World War Two – three of them at Chessington Zoo. The village, by now in the process of becoming a large residential area, received a good many hits.

On 2nd October 1940, a high explosive bomb fell on a shelter trench at 4.40am. Mrs Ernest George Arnold, aged 55, of The Lodge, Chessington Zoo, was killed, along with Ronald Page, aged eight, and his mother, Ann Page, both of the Cottage, Chessington Zoo. Roland's father survived but broke a leg.

Other bombs also fell on the zoo and are described on page 30. One blew off an ostrich's leg, another destroyed a monkey cage and penguin enclosure.

Some of the worst damage occurred at the recently-built Compton Crescent, Hemsby Road and Wilson Road.

On 1st July 1944, a pilot-less bomb – the doodlebug – buzzed over Chessington and by chance ran out of fuel over the housing estate built on the former Copt Gilders Farm. It exploded on impact with the rear of 28 Wilson Road, blowing up several houses in the neighbourhood.

Five-year-old David Tippett-Wilson, was sitting eating his breakfast in the kitchen of his parents' home at 159 Compton Crescent when the bomb went off.

He recalled: "We lost our roof. It was blown off in the blast. At the time I was a little boy sitting in the kitchen. The glass showered in over my 'egg soldiers' and chocolate. We lived at the bottom of Wilson Road, which was badly damaged, and the authorities came and put a tarpaulin over the roof

"I had to be evacuated to a Dr Barnado's home in Shropshire. Today, that house in Shropshire is used for training athletes for the Olympics.

"I went off by train with my little gas mask, and my mother *(Gwendoline)* came with me to Shropshire. I was picked up by a grey Barnado's lorry and taken to the house. I had a little dolly in my hand, and on my coat I had a luggage tag with my name and address. We all had those. There were about 100 of us and most were girls. In the gardens there were peacocks. We used to chase them and get told off."

David was later taken to live at a cousin's farm in Lincolnshire. "I got into trouble there because I left the farm gate open and the bull and chickens got out. And I fell into a dyke and almost drowned. A Polish farm worker pulled me out and since that time I've always had a good rapport with Poles.

A high explosive bomb virtually demolished nos. 9, 11, 13, and 15 Hemsby Road on 22nd October 1940. Fortunately there were no fatalities.

A flying bomb fell on to waste ground between Gilders Road and Church Lane on 4th July 1944, damaging theses cottages in Church Lane.

My mother went berserk when she got back to Chessington, the house was in such a state.

"My dad, (*Wilfred),* stayed at home and continued to cycle to work at Vickers in Weybridge, where he was an aircraft toolmaker.

"A year later, I remember soldiers coming up to us at The Stewponds, Epsom Common, and telling us the war was over."

Throughout the war years, families cheered each other up by putting on little shows on a home-made stage in Compton Crescent. These events proved great fun for the children – David's mother went on to run a nursery school from home.

The first recorded high explosive bomb to drop in Chessington was on 27th August 1940 at 2 Oak Cottages, almost opposite Byhurst Farm, Leatherhead Road. Much damage occurred. Another "HE" bomb dropped in a field north of Rushett Farm on the same day.

On 9th September the same year, an "HE" bomb fell at the rear of Park Cottages, south of the lane to Barwell Court Farm, but there was no damage here or at the Sir Francis Barker recreation ground from a similar device. The same day an unexploded bomb was reported at the same playing field.

On 27th September, four "HE" bombs came down but failed to cause damage at the Bonesgate Brickfields, Moor Lane, but windows were cracked when two "HE" devices detonated at the Sir Francis Barker field. The next day, The Cottage in Cox Lane was destroyed when it took a direct hit from an incendiary bomb. On 30th September, an "HE" bomb fell near the zoo

but there was no damage caused.

An unexploded bomb was reported by wardens two days later on the railway between Chessington South and North stations and in the front garden of 46 Stokesby Road and in the back garden of no. 9 – the same day the zoo fatalities – but there was no damage. Seven "HE" bombs dropped on Bunkers Hill, Leatherhead Road, again failing to cause interruption. On 4th October, two UXBs were discovered in fields at Rushett Lane, an "HE" went off and another bomb was reported. There was no damage.

On 7th October, a UXB was logged in the Leatherhead Road between Fairoak Lane and the Fox and Hounds as were two "HE" bombs in the same locality. Two other types of bomb fell here, too. Four days later, a device dropped in woods behind Gilders Road and an UXB was also removed.

An "HE" bomb blew a large crater in Leatherhead Road, 300 yards north of The Star on October 11th, while a UXB was taken away from a footpath near St Mary's Church.

On 12th October, there was slight damage to property when a bomb dropped on the Old Brightonians recreation ground. Two others dropped north of Chessington Zoo's driveway, both exploding. The next day, a "HE" bomb detonated in a field north of Roebuck Road.

Five days later, a bomb exploded in the tapir pen at the zoo, but there was no damage. Three "HE" bombs rocked the zoo vicinity and another "HE" went off on the railway embankment near the warden post at Chessington South.

Wilson Road and Compton Crescent after a doodlebug exploded on 1st July 1944. There were injuries but no one was killed. Both roads were named after the surnames of Chessington farmer Charles Moon's daughters when they married.

War diary

continued from page 50

Wardens based next to the Fairoak Brickyard reported that on 19th October 1940, two "HE" bombs exploded in fields west of Barwell Court, as well as another device.

Three days later, an "HE" bomb went off between the warden's post and trenches in Gilders Road, but there was no damage. On this day, the bomb fell on 13 and 15 Hemsby Road, leading to Nos.9,11,13 and 15 being demolished.

Additionally, two "HE" bombs and another device descended into fields at the rear of Gilders Road. Other HE bombs were reported 150 yards west of Leatherhead Road near Barwell and in fields at Byhurst Farm and 150 yards from Rushett Cottages.

On 25th October, a bomb caused slight damage to property north of Barwell Court while two others came down in a field next to the Sir Francis Barker Recreation ground.

Two "HE" bombs and another device went off in Acre Field, and two "HE" bombs exploded in a field north of Barwell Court Drive. Two "HE" bombs also fell in a field south of Gilders Road and Billockby Close. Next day, another HE bomb descended at the rear of 28 Roebuck Road.

On 6th November, three HE bombs were registered in fields north of Gilders Road and Billockby Close and two days later, three HE bombs were logged in fields south west of Byhurst Farm.

On 12th November, Leatherhead Road, 300 yards south of the zoo was partly blocked after an HE bomb exploded and another similar device led to sewers under the same road being damaged. Slight damage to property occurred at the corner of Bridge Road and Leatherhead Road when an "HE" went off but there was no damage to houses when other "HE" bombs exploded in a field north of Mansfield Road and two in fields at the rear of Woodall and Napier Farm.

The last day of November 1940 saw more attacks with an "HE" falling in a field 300 yards north of Rushett Lane and another in a field opposite Lotts Wood. Another two "HEs" fell at Rushett Farm.

The first bomb of 1941 came down opposite the Almshouses, Leatherhead Road on 11th January. The road was partly blocked and a water main damaged. Others fell near the zoo's kitchen gardens.

A renewed attack in 1943 saw anti-aircraft shells explode at the Ordnance Survey offices, where buildings were struck,

Two 265 buses serve the Copt Gilders estate about 1952. The first is destined for East Acton. The Ruxford Stores, Co-op, a fruit and vegetable shop and Peberdy's newsagents can be made out. The newsagent's also housed the Gilders Road post office. By the 1990s, the post office and newsagent's had gone and there were fewer shops in the parade than when it was built in the early 1930s after Copt Gilders Hall Farm and its land had been sold for extensive housing.

and at Fleetwood, where nearby properties suffered from blast damage.

An unexploded anti-aircraft bomb was reported at Roebuck Road on 16th June 1944.

Then came the 1944 doodlebugs' onslaught – on 21st June near Chessington Woods, and another near Cox Lane. On 23rd June, one damaged the zoo's miniature railway and another Acre Hill Farm. The same day another fell in Chessington Woods. The most damaging "buzz" bombs, as described earlier, were at Wilson Road on 1st July and at the zoo on 19th July, where there were three fatalities. Yet another fly bomb damaged properties off Cox Lane on 23rd July.

Before the war, rural Cox Lane seemed like miles from anywhere. There was White's farm locals used to call "Nowhere"

A tea break at the Bailey family's Rushett Dairy Farm in the 1930s.

Annie Bailey in the 1950s at Byhurst Farmhouse.

Byhurst farm

BYHURST Farm, Leatherhead Road, is centuries old, but the present three-storey farmhouse dates back only to 1916. Seventeeth century maps describe it as Byers Farm.

On 5th November 1939, the Bailey family from Rushett Dairy Farm, opposite, took it over and stayed for three decades. The farm had been empty for 13 years as the land was earmarked for a Welwyn Garden City-type new town. It was never built. A shopping parade was planned at Fairoak crossroads, a few yards north of the Fairoak Lane junction and concrete foundations can still be found below undergrowth just north of the traffic lights. This all fitted in well with the scheme to extend the railway southwards to Leatherhead from Chessington South.

The foundations of the earlier farmhouse can be detected near the pond. The farm used to be owned by the Star Omnibus Company and was apparently used for stabling horses on stage-coach runs at one time.

In the mid-1970s, widower Fred Blake kept cattle at Byhurst.

Harvest time in the fields at Byhurst Farm in the late 1940s. In the war years, Margaret Bailey used to ring a loud bell to warn the farm labourers of air raids.

Villagers earning some "beer money" haymaking at Byhurst Farm in the 1940s.

North Parade

NORTH Parade was built, along with Chessington North Station, in 1937-8.

The shops included Whitfords, the newsagent's, where children spent many happy hours choosing Dinky toys and sweets. It was *the* place to buy fireworks for Guy Fawkes night.

Whitfords was still trading at the same premises in 1999.

Another "old-timer" was Edanas, the wool shop, on the opposite side. In the 1970s, one of the shop staff was Joan Easton who had previously run the Little Shop in Clayton Road, Hook.

The parade housing Edanas was built in the 1950s and included Rumblelows where, in the 1960s, hit parade singles could be bought. This site used to be wasteland where fairs with swinging boats and coconut shies were held. Youngsters loved go-karting those days and risked life or limb as they hurtled down the nearby roads.

Fairoak Stores and post office

Frank Clarke, pictured above, took over Fairoak Stores and sub post office with his wife, Bertha, and daughter, Joan, in 1956. It was in the family's hands until 1967. Also in the photograph is one of the regular postmen, emptying the pillar box outside. In 1999, the shop had been gone for about eight years and items of food were available only from the BP garage.

Lion goes on shopping trip
The Clarkes

BY 1930, Fairoak Stores, on the corner of Leatherhead Road and Rushett Lane, was open as a sub post office and general stores. It replaced the little Chessington post office and stores on the other side of the Leatherhead Road, next to the brickworks, which was run by the Sayers family.

In the 1930s, Fairoak Stores was run by James William Pywell. By 1934, another PO had opened up in Gilders Road, on the new Copt Gilders estate.

Fairoak Stores was taken over in 1956 by Frank and Bertha Clarke, who bought it from a Mr and Mrs Roberts. The Clarkes' daughter, Joan, worked in the shop, becoming sub postmistress before the family sold the business in 1967.

On one occasion, Joan, accompanied by her father, used her Ford Anglia to chase fraudsters. With Joan at the wheel, the criminals were pursued to Sutton. They were later charged by the police and convicted in court.

"Classy" Kunzle cakes were a speciality at the shop, recalled Joan, who delivered newspapers to the village on horseback. Joan married a David Clark – Clark without an "e" – and years later spent her retirement at Mid Holmwood, near Dorking.

Joan Clarke with her dog, Boz, in 1959, and below, on her horse, delivering newspapers.

Bertha Clarke and Boz, the Airedale which sat outside the shop, greeting customers.

Bertha Clarke served lunchtime teas to the Windsor factory staff.

Chessington Zoo's director, Mr Snazle, kept a young lion at his home in West Road in the 1960s, and zoo staff sometimes took it shopping in Fairoak Stores.

Blue Peter's Valerie Singleton visits Chessington

IT seemed to be a favourite media trick, taking big cats for walks to the village post office at Chessington.

Following the young lion's visit in 1967, which "co-incided" with a press photographer's appearance, the BBC got in on the act the following year.

Millions of young viewers watched Blue Peter presenter, Valerie Singleton, walk up Leatherhead Road from the West Road direction with the lion, Valentine, pulling hard on a lead.

After a battle to get the creature inside the store, Miss Singleton managed to remain calm as the zoo animal playfully leapt up at her and on to the counter.

Cameramen homed in on the Lyons cake sign outside and also at Valentine being offered some Lyons syrup, which may or may not have been consumed.

In the mid 1970s, John and Marjorie Martin took over the store with help from Sylvia Budd.

Quickly, they became well-liked in the village, but they were beset by poor health.

Sadly, Mrs Martin was widowed in 1998 when John died suddenly at their home near the Chessington Computer Centre.

Sylvia Budd had died some years earlier. New owners ran the shop and post office in the 1980s, but in 1989 it closed, but not for good. It briefly reopened as a general store but without a post office or newsagents, it proved unviable.

The entrance to Chessington Zoo in 1968.

Blue Peter's Valerie Singleton inside the Fairoak Stores, Chessington, in 1968.

The lion is "given" some golden syrup with a lion trademark

Valerie Singleton struggles with the young lion outside the Fairoak Stores, Leatherhead Road.

A surprised shopkeeper at Fairoak Stores in 1968 serves Valerie Singleton and keeps a wary eye on Valentine the lion as the creature jumps up on the counter.

Chamberlain, King, Queen and Kennedy in Hook

US Ambassador Joseph Kennedy, recalled to America by Roosevelt in 1941, with Prime Minister Neville Chamberlain at RAF Hook in 1939.

King George VI and Queen Elizabeth (the future Queen Mother) being greeted at RAF Hook, Mansfield Road, on 16th April 1939. Well-wishers lined the streets to welcome the royal visitors.

R AF Chessington started its life as RAF Hook Balloon Barrage Station in 1938 – the year before the outbreak of the Second World War.

A 45-acre site on the Chessington side of Mansfield Road, Hook, was used to build the base in the year Chamberlain signed the Munich Agreement with Hitler. The fields were part of the vast Lovelace estate when it was purchased by the Air Ministry in October 1937 to form one of 10 barrage balloon centres in and around London.

The site was to have 50 balloons from which dangled steel cables from a height of 25,000ft to stop raiding aircraft approaching at low altitudes.

Recruitment began in May 1938 for the two Territorial Air Service squadrons, 904 and 905, to be stationed at Hook as part of the Auxiliary Air Force rather than the regular RAF.

Building work on hangars began in the spring of 1938 and the RAF officially took over in the August.

The importance of the low profile station was suddenly magnified after a surprise visit by VIPs on 16th April 1939. King George VI and Queen Elizabeth (who became the Queen Mother), together with Prime Minister Neville Chamberlain and the US Ambassador, Joseph Kennedy (father of J F Kennedy), toured the site. The dignitaries had driven from Windsor for the visit.

Crowds lined the Hook Road to welcome the royal visitors to Hook. "Many cottages and houses were gaily decorated with flags and bunting and thousands of people thronged the roads to get a glimpse of the royal party," reported the Surrey Comet.

Some 1,200 auxiliaries and 200 regular RAF men were on parade for the occasion at which closely guarded barrage secrets were revealed to the special guests. Celia Collins, the young daughter of Mr and Mrs L Collins, of Hemsby Road, unsuccessfully tried to hand the Queen a bouquet.

The King, and Queen Elizabeth, the future Queen Mother, tours the RAF base during her visit to Hook in 1939. A barrage balloon hangs above.

RAF Chessington, off Mansfield Road, in the 1980s.

RAF Hook continued to operate barrage balloons throughout the Second World War. After hostilities ceased, in 1945, the base became a medical equipment depot and an RAF medical rehabilitation unit.

RAF patients with disabilities were brought there to learn new skills and be trained in how to overcome their handicaps.

The base was expanded in 1968 to take in patients from the army and navy as well.

After being renamed RAF Chessington, it became the only centre in the country to cater for all the armed services. Only patients from the bottom four ranks were brought in. Others went elsewhere.

For nearly 20 years the base continued in this role, as a joint services medical rehabilitation unit.

Then, in 1984, came an announcement that it was to close, swiftly followed by the news that the US Army was to take it over.

The Americans wanted the base as a peacetime medical storage depot and a wartime hospital.

Considerable arrangements were put in place to make the latter possible.

At first there was a local outcry over the US Army's plans, but the scheme went ahead.

The rehabilitation unit was transferred to RAF Headley Court, near Leatherhead, and the site was turned over to the 47th Area Support Group to become a 1,000-bed hospital, ready to be activated for NATO use in wartime.

Eighty six, 40-ton lorries shipped the £10m worth of medical equipment to the base and the final touches to the hospital were put in place during 1988.

In October 1987, the public were invited to inspect the NATO exercises carried out that month and during two weeks of the following few years until the base was closed in the early 1990s.

Roads on the estate built on the site are named after the men of Hook and Chessington who lost their lives in the First and Second World Wars.

Hilda Coppard at Coppard Gardens on the housing estate built on the former RAF base. The road commemorates her brother, Bill, (inset) killed in service in Italy during the Second World War.

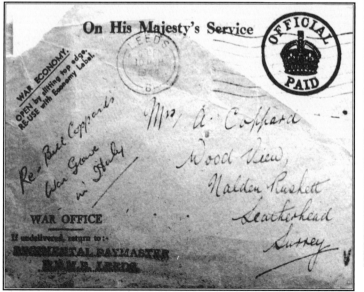

Letter sent to Hilda Coppard's mother at Wood View, Malden Rushett, with news of her son's war grave.

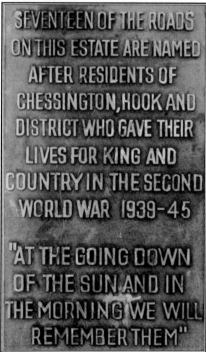

SEVENTEEN OF THE ROADS ON THIS ESTATE ARE NAMED AFTER RESIDENTS OF CHESSINGTON, HOOK AND DISTRICT WHO GAVE THEIR LIVES FOR KING AND COUNTRY IN THE SECOND WORLD WAR 1939-45

"AT THE GOING DOWN OF THE SUN AND IN THE MORNING WE WILL REMEMBER THEM"

Plaque erected in the 1990s at Coppard Gardens on the former RAF site.

St Philip's School and Fleetwood house

St Philip's School which used to be a house with a variety of names.

STRAWBERRY Hill, Chessington Place, Fleetwood and St Philip's School are names given over the years to the large house off Leatherhead Road, that started life in about 1700 as a smaller house called, curiously, Shrinreltonten.

By 1800 it had become a substantial residence known as Strawberry Hill. The curate of Chessington, Rev Lewis, lived there in the early 1850s. By the turn of the century, its name had changed to Chessington Place and the Monier Williams family lived there for 30 years until 1918. Mr M F Monier Williams was the grandson of Colonel Monier Williams, Surveyor General of the Bombay Presidency.

The house's large meadows at the front, which extended to The Harrow, used to be reaped by the Stickley farmers. By 1932, and up until 1954, it was known as Fleetwood. In the 1930s, the house's occupiers were the Mitford family. W Bertram Mitford (who drove a Rolls Royce and had a chauffeur) and Emily Cecil Mitford were in residence. Their two boys were described as "mischievous" by former housekeepers. Frank B Mitford was killed in the Second World War. His name is recalled in Mitford Close on the former RAF camp housing estate off Mansfield Road.

St Philip's School opened on 3rd May 1954 under headmistress Miss F A Lloyd. There were 11 special needs pupils catered for.

By June 1954, the roll had increased to 37 in three classes. It was estimated that 35 tons of coke were needed per year for heating the school.

A log book from the summer of 1954 states: "Children are producing gooseberries, bringing orders from home, weighing up the orders, taking money and giving change."

By September 1954, 46 pupils were on the roll. Bonfire celebrations were being planned and four guinea pigs were purchased.

The school roll had increased to 80 by January 1955 and by March of the same year, plans were underway to improve the entrance to the school by demolishing Fleetwood Lodge at the gateway and widening the drive.

In February 1960, there were school visits to see the film Ben Hur, Bentalls store in Kingston, the Royal Mills at Esher and the seaside at Littlehampton.

The same year, an article appeared in a Surbiton magazine quoting the memories of a former footman at the house in bygone times.

It raised a few eyebrows because it stated that in the 1930s the house was owned by Nancy Mitford, who some took to be the famous sister of Diana Mitford, the Nazi sympathiser. A study of Nancy and Diana Mitford's family tree gives no obvious link to Chessington's Bertram and Emily Mitford.

Old vicarage and parsonage

Charles Moon, a farmer, of Chessington Court (now Holmwood Road estate), gave his house in Church Lane to St Mary's Church in 1939 to replace the old parsonage next to the church. The 'Moon' vicarage was demolished in the 1970s and flats built on the site.

ALTHOUGH Chessington's church is more than 800 years old, it has only had its own vicar since 1938, when its ancient links with Malden were finally severed. Before then, the Malden-based vicar was in charge of both parishes, although a curate lived at Chessington. In late Victorian times, the vicar, Reverend Chetwynd Staplyton, walked up to 14 miles on a Sunday, conducting services. "I used to walk to Malden Rushett to take an evening of cottage lectures,

A plaque on the former Church Lane vicarage.

beginning at the Church Room *(next to the Star)* and then on to a cottage near the brickfield, then on to Chessington School, thus getting in three meetings on one evening walking home by 10pm," he said.

In 1969, a new vicarage was built on the site of the old parsonage next door to the church. Its first occupants were Rev Christopher Fowles, his wife, Pat, and family.

The old parsonage next to the church.

'A village atmosphere so near to London'

St Mary's School, 1970

A COUNTRY village school atmosphere still prevailed at St Mary's, Leatherhead Road, as late as the early 1970s. In the summer of 1970, a reporter from the Kingston Borough News visited the pupils and the headmaster, Mr Philip Rowe, too see how the little school of just four classrooms was getting along in a world which was rapidly changing.

Reporter, Carolyn Humphreys, found out there were just 110 pupils and that it seemed "incredible" there was alive and well a village school "so close to London".

Mr Rowe told the newspaper: "We have a marked family atmosphere in the school despite the varied backgrounds of the pupils."

The reporter was told how the introduction of electric heating into the classrooms was relatively recent, and up to the late 1950s, the boys and girls were warmed only by open fires in the classrooms.

"The problem with open fires was that the children in the front roasted and the others could not get warm," Mr Rowe said at the time.

Pupils seemed to be enjoying a wide variety of lessons. Some had been studying an ants' nest and the behaviour of the insects. The children were encouraged to do as much creative writing as possible and they were not restricted to formal grammar.

Poems by the children were on display and Mr Rowe commented: "It is really surprising that young children can create such beautiful and thoughtful work."

Pupils often went on trips to places such as the Isle of Wight, Portsmouth and Winchester and they had enjoyed camping under canvas.

The Nuffield method of teaching maths was employed, but most parents did not understand it so Mr Rowe gave mothers and fathers a lesson to put this right.

The flexible headmaster could also turn his hand to teaching French to the youngsters.

An active parent-teacher association gave much help to the school.

By now, however, the school was suffering from a lack of space, but Mr Rowe had grand plans to extend the cloakrooms and flatten a small field at the rear of the school to create a junior playground. The school did have the use of the recreation ground next door. The ground was sold to the cricket club some years earlier on condition that St Mary's could use it as required.

The school, built in 1865, still had no assembly room, but the next-door Chessington parish hall was used for school dinners, assembly and musical events. The meals were thankfully prepared at the premises, Mr Rowe pointed out.

For 21 years Mrs Vera Sheath shepherded the pupils of St Mary's School across the busy Leatherhead Road. In July 1970, (the month Mungo Jerry were at the top of the pop charts with In the Summertime), she decided to retire. Inset: Headmaster Philip Rowe.

An 'RM' 65 bus en route from Chessington Zoo to Ealing in about 1977 stops at the Lucky Rover, Hook. The 65 first served Chessington on 1st December 1924 when the route went daily from Ealing (Argyle Road) to Leatherhead (The Bull). It replaced the 105A which ran from Ealing to Leatherhead from 24th May 1914, chiefly on Sundays only. Copt Gilders was first served by the 265 (from May 1952 to New Year's Eve 1966) after which the service was replaced by the 65A and then the 71. The 71's debut run to Chessington was on 30th November 1968 and by 1987 had completely taken over from the 65.

An RT-model 65 bus to Chessington Zoo in the early 1970s. The RTs and RMs were staffed with a driver and conductor.

Some of the girls at Chessington St Mary's Church of England School on a winter's day in 1976 – the year which experienced a tremendous heatwave with temperatures in the 80s and 90sF for days on end. Crops on Rushett Farm and elsewhere were stunted as the seemingly endless days of hot sunshine beat down on the fields.

Fleetwood School

FLEETWOOD School was opened in Garrison Lane in 1954. The name reflected the large house which stood close by. It catered as a secondary school for the growing population of post-war Chessington.

Headmaster Harry Blasby retired in July 1989 after 21 years in the post. Thereafter, the school became Chessington Community College. Mr Blasby is pictured above in the week he retired.

Ellingham schooldays

ELLINGHAM School opened as Garrison Lane New County Primary Junior on 13th June 1955, off Ellingham Road, under the headship of Mr S G Evans with his staff of Mr D Stott, Mrs R Soff, Mrs M Prescott and Miss M Wraight. One hundred and sixty nine children were admitted in the first week. Then, school dinners were provided by Moor Lane central kitchen. Mrs Lynn and Mrs Le Pavoux served the dinners on the first day. In 1984 Mr Ian Jones was appointed head and still held the post in 1999.

Fred Eames, (right) of Green Lane, was a Jack of all trades. He kept animals and often had battles with the local council. He used to sell fish from a cart.

'Tarzan' lived rough in woods

TARZAN was a rough man who lived in a tin shed in the woods at Green Lane at the foot of a duck farm.

He washed in the stream and it is said he ate blackbirds and woodpigeons and dug graves for cash at St Mary's Church. It is said he obtained beer money by selling small items of jewellery such as gold rings.

He was in the army in the Great War and seemed to know how to live in the wild. People vividly recall his dirty skin and his love of a drink in the Blackamoor's Head. Once he gave a schoolboy a 10s note when he'd been drinking only to ask for it back the next day. He died in the 1950s.

Ellingham schoolchildren in 1980.

A Morris Marina approaches the Leatherhead Road roundabout in the 1970s while an RT bus makes a stop in Hook. Chessington has changed dramatically since the building boom of the '30s, '40s and '50s. Many clubs, societies and sports groups have thrived in the modern communities. Chessington library, Moor Lane, opened in April 1933, but in recent years amalgamated with Hook; the Methodist Church opened in the same road along with the Evangelical Church in Parbury Rise, now relocated to the Kings Centre. The Catholic church of St Catherine of Sienna opened in 1938 with clergy supplied by Our Lady Immaculate, Tolworth, but taking on its own priest, Father Kelly, in 1945. A new church was built in 1975 at the site.

Chessington and Hook experienced the second heaviest rainfall ever to have been recorded in a day in the Greater London area. The great storm, on Friday 6th July 1973 left more than 300 homes and North Parade (above) under water. Victor Dorling, of Bolton Road, recorded 4.6 ins of rain.

IN the mid 1970s, plans to relocate St Mary's School to new premises in Church Lane were realised with much support provided by parents.

The old school was demolished and four smart town houses were built on the site.

1999

1958

Lovelace School's primary department was opened at Mansfield Road, Hook, in 1952, and the junior section two years later. Here are some of those watching the maypole dancing in 1958.

Moor Lane School opened in 1936 to cope with the huge population boost as a result of the new housing estates in Chessington. Singer Petula Clark, who lived in Salmons Road, was a pupil. Here are some of the staff from recent years under Mrs Jane Wright's headship.

About the author

MARK Davison has had a keen interest in local history all his life. His enthusiasm for the subject was greatly encouraged by the Kingston Borough News columnist and historian, Margaret Bellars, who helped him join the newspaper's staff when he left school.

Mark was brought up in Bramham Gardens, Hook, and went to St Paul's School, where, at the age of 11, he produced a newsy school magazine with the help of friends.

His career in journalism took him to Epsom, Redhill, Buxton and then Reigate, where he is currently community editor of the Surrey Mirror.

He has passionately campaigned to keep the two identities of Hook and Chessington separate and persuaded large stores to support him. He was delighted when a new signboard outside the post office in Hook Parade carried the words: Hook Post Office, underlining, at last, that Hook and Chessington are two 'villages' steeped in history even if their borders are sometimes ambiguous to newcomers.

Other books

Among other books by the same author are:

Hook Remembered. Published by Frosted Earth. £9.95 (ISBN 0-9516710-9-x)

Long Ditton Remembered. Published by Mark Davison. £9.95 (ISBN 0-9534240-0-6)

Surrey Weather Book. Published by Frosted Earth. £9.95 (ISBN 0-9516710-6-5)

Surrey in the Sixties. Published by Frosted Earth. £12.95 (ISBN 0-9516710-4-9)

Surrey in the Seventies. Published by Frosted Earth. £9.95 (ISBN 0-9516710-7-3)

Surrey in the Hurricane. Published by Froglets £8.50. (ISBN 0-9513019-2-6)

London's Hurricane. Published by Froglets. £8.50. (ISBN 0-9513019-8-5)

Singer Petula Clark receives a signed copy of Hook Remembered from the author, Mark Davison, in September 1998. She spent some of her childhood living at Salmons Road, Chessington, and attended Moor Lane School. She once sang "Ave Maria" from the balcony of Barwell Court at a garden party during the Second World War. Asked about her Moor Lane schooldays, she said: "I was really good at nothing at school but I suppose literature, if anything. Maths? No! Anything to do with maths, no!"